Books by Richard Louv

The Web of Life
FatherLove
101 Things You Can Do For Our Children's Future
Childhood's Future
America II

The Web
of Life

The Web of Life

Weaving the Values
that Sustain Us

Richard Louv

Conari Press
Berkeley, CA

Cover Design: Nita Ybarra Design

Conari Press books are distributed by Publishers Group West

Library of Congress Cataloging-in-Publication Data

Louv, Richard.
The web of life : weaving the values that sustain us / Richard Louv.
    p.   cm.
ISBN 1-57324-036-2 (hardcover)
    1. Meditations.   I. Title
BL624.2.L68   1996
814'.54–dc20   95-51847

Printed in the United States of America on recycled paper.
10 9 8 7 6 5 4 3 2 1

Man did not weave the web of life.
He is merely a strand in it.
Whatever he does to the web
he does to himself.

–Chief Seattle

The Web of Life

Weaving . . . 2

THE STRAND OF COMMUNITY

THE STRAND OF NATURE

THE STRAND OF TIME

THE STRAND OF SPIRIT

To the memory of Lucy Hollembeak

Weaving

VISUALIZE THE WEB OF YOUR LIFE, intricate and mysterious. The web is there for us all; all of us are weavers. For children, one strand is made of parents, another is the school system, another is the work place and how it treats parents, another is the neighborhood. But all of us, no matter how young or old, need a web of family, friendship, community, nature, time, and spirit.

In our culture, this weaving is a kind of lost art, awaiting rediscovery.

Consider the strands. In current times, the web has become our most powerful ecological image. Scientists no longer talk of the food chain, but of the food web. Each organism's life cycle is intertwined with the lives of all other organisms. But, of course, the image predates science. The image of the circular, interconnected structure of social, psychological and spiritual health appears in nearly every culture's mythology. Long ago, Chief Seattle said, whatever man "does to the web he does to himself."

Black Elk, an Oglala Sioux holy man who witnessed the destruction of his people during the mid-1880s, described his vision of the web, which he called the nation's hoop, this way:

"I was standing on the highest mountain of them all, and round about beneath me was the whole hoop of the world . . . . And I saw that the sacred hoop of my people was one of many hoops that made one circle, wide as daylight and starlight, and in the center grew one mighty flowering tree to shelter all the children of one mother and one father. And I saw that it was holy."

Later, he described the loss of his nation's hoop—how "all the marching animals grew restless and afraid that they were not what they had been, and began sending forth voices of trouble, calling to their chiefs," how he looked down and saw "that the leaves were falling from the holy tree . . . all the animals and fowls that were the people ran here and there, for each one seemed to have his own little vision that he followed and his own rules; and all over the universe I could hear the winds at war like wild beasts fighting." The nation's hoop was "broken like a ring of smoke that spreads and scatters and the holy tree seemed dying and all its birds were gone."

And another image of the web, much older: The prophet Isaiah, circa 730 B.C., wrote, "There is One Who is dwelling above the circle of the earth, the dwellers of which are as grasshoppers, the One Who is stretching out the heavens just as a fine gauze, Who spreads them out like a tent in which to dwell."

In our society, it is easy to lose sight of the web. To mend our hoop, our protective gauze, we must envision the whole ecology and not only the parts. Yet, even in the dark, we can find the faithful remnants and begin to weave. And as our hands hold the strands, the strands begin to hold us.

In a previous book, *Childhood's Future,* I described the new web that must be woven to support children;

this book furthers that theme, but shifts the emphasis to other passages of our lives.

For many years, as a columnist for *The San Diego Union-Tribune*, I have been drawn to people who are acutely aware of the web, even if they call it by other names. In Kansas, a woman in her nineties, who is God's friend but asks nothing of Him; a Chippewa chaplin who liberates prisoners through a burning doorway in time and space; a woman in Oregon who has found her one true place; a Navajo flutist who helps people listen to their inner voices—and my wife and children and friends and many others who teach me daily about the connections of time and spirit.

This book is a collection of thoughts, theirs and mine, about the web in our lives, and our lives in the web.

The Strand
of Family

Although it is made of thin, delicate strands, the web is not easily broken. However, a web gets torn every day by the insects that kick around in it, and a spider must rebuild it when it gets full of holes.

–E.B. White

The Little Things

THE LITTLE THINGS. The click of your wife's makeup bottles and brushes in the bathroom in the morning, the sub-surface sound of them, a kind of music. The accompaniments: the older boy's bedroom door opening and shutting in haste, a faucet running, a gust of wind in the eucalyptus, the last rain on the window. The little things are what we remember, what we know, of family life. Of life.

The large events have their place, but even the large events of a family's passage are assembled from little things. The rush to the emergency room and the way the air feels there and the brave little chin thrust up beneath the mask, the small choked cry and the sound—especially this sound—of the thread being pulled through the wound, and the way the little hand holds tight to your finger. The little things.

Without realizing it, we can neglect the little things.

Though I have never divorced and my vow is for life, I have like most people experienced a broken relationship or two. Grief does not attach itself so much to the empty space left by the other person, a loss often too abstract to grasp, but to the little things. The vertical space in the closet where familiar clothes once hung. The smell on the pillow or, on the street, a stranger's accent that conjures up a silenced voice.

When our parents and loved ones die, little things

come back. Returning home after a death, you find a quilt that wrapped around you long ago, and you remember how the hands felt as they tucked you in. You find yourself startled by the way the dishes are arranged in your parent's kitchen cabinet; you are surprised because you know the arrangement, and you did not know it was so familiar until you looked at it within the context of loss.

The impression most remembered from my grandmother's death is not of the large fact of her body in the casket, but of coming into her cold kitchen a few days afterward and seeing the jar of mincemeat cookies, which she often made for me and my brother. In the jar, then, they were covered with mold.

Just as family grief is articulated by little things, so is joy. Here is an exercise: Go through your house when everyone is away and, in the silence, look for these little things.

In my house, I see the drawing of Wyoming with the owl in the tree singing, "Ho, ho, ho," and the little wooden toolbox, with the name Matt carved on the side, filled with crayons, some of them peeled. The smell of them connects you in time. The crumbs on top of the toaster, the empty cereal boxes left out, seem suddenly precious. So do the stacks of games—*Candyland, Clue, Monopoly*. Each family's *Monopoly* is stamped with its unique patina of worn corners and stained Chance cards. Little things.

The fishing rods leaning against the corner of the garage, some from my own childhood, some bought for the boys. The rods stand tall together. Shelves filled with books; most of them old, neglected friends, each with a story to tell.

A balsa glider on the stairs. At the top of the landing, a small landscape, a stop-time mountain scene painted in oils by the boys' grandfather. Once, twice, the bullfrog in my older son's room harrumphs, because spring is coming; in a distant time, when my sons or my wife or I, alone or together, drive past some stream or pond surrounded by reeds shaking with redwing blackbirds, we will hear this particular booming sound and in it recognize these years of our family life.

In the largest bedroom, the smell of a comforter; and in the closet, my wife's clothing hangs neat and fresh. And all around the room the bottles of roses, which she has carefully dried over seventeen years, all the roses I have given, not one missed. And beside the bathtub a thick, red, scented candle with lots of time left in it.

Here is the next part of this exercise: When your family is home again, listen to them, watch them, wait for the sounds and smells and tilted chins and the shouted competitions between the children and the sighs of the house as it slips into sleep. Hold these things. These little things are everything.

Chains do not hold a marriage together. It is threads, hundreds of tiny threads which sew people together through the years.

—Simone Signoret

The Essence of Family

MEMORY, IT SEEMS TO ME, IS THE ESSENCE OF FAMILY; the longer and deeper the memory, the stronger the family. By stronger I do not necessarily mean better. Just stronger.

I was talking to a friend the other day about memory. We were sharing a feeling that we both have had, but seldom discuss, that we are the bearers of our parents, the vessels that hold the images and sounds and touch of them.

"Nobody will ever have the memories of my family that I have," my friend said. "Sometimes it gets almost creepy weird that a sound, a smell, will set it off—will almost bring the spirit back, and at times I do feel the presence of my parents."

But what happens when the vessel breaks, when I am no longer around to remember? Do these ashes of memory disappear?

I am thankful that I can call my brother on the telephone, sometimes late at night; I am here and he is in Eureka, but we can walk across old ground together. Sometimes, walking across this old ground, we see our parents approaching. Of course, my brother and I do not see them with the same eyes, but rather with a kind of overlapping stereo vision. At the very least, our sharing brings into more vivid relief the people and landscapes of the past.

But memory is tricky. Scientists are often amazed at the faithfulness of memory, but their studies have shown memory to be both powerful and fragile, constantly reshuffling and gradually decaying in the brain. We tend to remember best what we have experienced in stress or intense emotion; this means that the expanse of our memory does not accurately reflect the fullness of our pasts. Moreover, "source amnesia" is common; we can recall a fact or anecdote but cannot remember where we learned it. Source memories are the quickest to decay.

When I think about the fragility of my memory, that it will not only disappear someday but that it is already changing, I am filled with both fear and relief. Fear that I may lose my memory; relief that, rather than dying, my memory will, in a sense, lead a life of its own, and therefore can live on without me.

I remember, in the 1970s, sitting at a table in a dimly lit room on the Northern Cheyenne reservation with Marie Sanchez, a tribal judge and firebrand. Surrounded by her family, holding her grandchild tightly wrapped, she told me about her great-great-grandfather, Little Wolf, the Cheyenne chief who, in the late 1800s, led his people out of forced confinement in Oklahoma back to their native country in what is now Montana. She told how, for thousands of miles, Little Wolf and his people had evaded U.S. soldiers by building sweat lodges, entering them, and emerging hundreds of miles away.

To Sanchez, this story of spiritual transport was absolutely true, historically and personally. As she told it, surrounded by extended family and tribe, she often used the words "we" and "I," as if she had been a participant in the long escape. This is one of the traits of mythic memory; not trapped in time or place, it becomes our own. Orally, this story had been passed down for a century, and it had never lost its power. It had, in fact, lived and grown.

In my culture, though, memory does not live as easily. Most of us are not surrounded by extended family or tribe; we are more nomadic and fragmented than even the most traditionally nomadic tribes, and our personal memories compete with an overpowering, never-ending onslaught of information. As a result, it is too easy to discount our family memories. Not enough action. The plots are obscure. No name actors.

Still, my memories and yours are unique. There is nothing like them in the world. Each set is a work of neurological art. If I owned a Picasso, I would not leave it out in the rain. The memories we carry should be treated with as much respect. We should find somewhere safe to put our memories, and the safest place is not in our own vessel, because it will inevitably break.

The way to preserve our memories is to make gifts of them. We make our collections of videotape and Kodachrome; we keep diaries; we write family histories; we pass on family stories to our children and to what we can muster of a tribe of friends, and we call our brothers and sisters late at night and walk old ground with them. And the memories, like children with lives of their own, move on.

Preserving Our Stories

OUR STORIES, OUR PERSONAL STORIES, our family stories, are our real gold. If we're lucky, as we age, we put our stories in the bank, where they gather interest, in deepening meaning.

"As I grew up, I loved listening to my grandparents' stories," a friend, Liz, told me recently. "I was drawn to their calm and intrigued by the scope of their lives. I remember my grandmother telling stories about my Great-Aunt Ag, who once modeled camisoles and ladies' undergarments."

Today, Liz's family members rarely tell stories.

Somehow we assume that if a story isn't in the video store or on TV, it must not be worth much.

"One evening I was baby-sitting the nine-year-old daughter of a friend. This little girl loves to hear about her mother's life. So she asked me to tell her a story about my childhood, and I was struck with panic. I couldn't think of a thing. I know I have stories. But here was a child asking me for something so simple as a story and I couldn't think of one.

"I learned two things that night. One was that I had lost touch with the stories I grew up with; and two, I'm not making many new stories. Maybe the lives we lead today are mind-numbing, and not the source of many good stories. A lot of the stuff of good stories has to do with family life and we have precious little time for that now."

It's tough to live good stories when you're stuck in traffic.

Author Rexford Brown contends that true literacy is impossible without the ability to value and tell our stories. Brown describes a Navajo school, where one-third of the children come to class illiterate in two languages, English and their native tongue, an indirect, storytelling language that is fading from the culture.

At the reservation he studied, a medicine man stood up at a school board meeting and told a story about twins, one crippled, the other blind: the blind one carries the crippled one, and the crippled one guides them with his eyes; both of them are looking for signs to give their lives meaning and end their wandering. Together, they make their story.

The medicine man went on to attack the schools for neglecting the native language, and for failing to realize that Navajo children have traditionally learned through experience, not books or videos or computers. And he chastised his own Navajo people for losing touch with their inheritance of stories and legends.

In a sense, all over America, children are losing their inheritance. They're bused long distances to what amount to educational reservations: schools colonized by bureaucratic story-killing language, schools too often cut off from neighborhood or family. But there are exceptions. "I did find a teacher in Kentucky who created a coal curriculum," Brown says. "He took everything back to square one, and related every part of the class study to coal and to miners: this is what we know. We know coal. Kids need context."

So do the rest of us.

Mental hospitals and our parks are populated with people who have lost their stories or their connection to other people's stories. Nonetheless there seems to be a growing hunger out there. The reaction to the PBS *Civil War* series is an example of how starved people are for powerful, authentic stories about real people, about ourselves and our legacies. And the new popularity of salons—where people get together to do that most radical of acts, talk face-to-face—suggests the hunger.

A college friend, Jewell Scott of Kansas City, told me about a special recent evening, in which her friends' family stories came together. "I was invited to a party to which each person brought their favorite childhood food. The evening began with exclamations over the various dishes —homemade macaroni and real cheese, salmon patties and apple pie and chocolate chip cookies. One dish was cooked right at the party in an authentic, 1960s vintage, Harvest Gold electric skillet."

"What is it?" everyone asked. They peered into the layers of sliced red potatoes with shredded cheese and crumbled bacon, crowned with eggs poaching in the melting cheese.

"It's 'potato stuff,'" the cook responded.

The group reveled in the old-fashioned tastes of real eggs, butter, animal fat, sugar, and cholesterol. After the last apple pie and ice cream had been eaten and they had discussed whether it was better to eat well and live long or eat "good" and die young, the talk returned to their childhoods, their families, and their feelings about them.

Though they had known one another for years, they

had never shared these stories, and what they learned was remarkable. "Three of us were descended from circuit-riding ministers who brought the Gospel to the wild Midwest of the mid-to late 1800s. One grandmother had lived in the northern plains. From Texas to Canada, these great-grandparents we remembered had seen their world change from saddles and shotguns and lonely prairies to electric lights, central air conditioning, and jet travel.

"Our own parents merited our respect for their experiences in the Great Depression and World War II and for rearing their children through a time of incredible rebellion against them and their values. As we sat on the redwood deck, sipping our Chablis and watching a police helicopter cut through the starlit urban sky, we marveled at the legacies they share and how we so rarely talk about them."

The group yearned a bit for the simpler days of "potato stuff" and visits to their grandparents to hear them spin stories of a different time and place. They wondered whether they would live to be eighty or ninety or one hundred, and laughed about how many years the evening's meal had subtracted from their lives.

"And, finally, the evening ended without any conclusion to the most important question: Would we bring to our old age a sense of humor, patience and kindness that would make us lovable, likable human beings and, someday, thirty or forty or fifty years from now, would there be any reason for another group of party-goers to remember us and our incredible lives?"

When children are asked to define family, they are more forgiving than many adults, and more accurate.

Valeria Lovelace, Sesame Street's director of research, asked children to define family. Children, in her study, were most likely to identify "Mr. and Mrs. Brown and Billy" as a family. "However, later on in the interviews," says Lovelace, "we said Mr. and Mrs. Brown and Billy live together but they don't love each other. Are they a family?" Half the children who had earlier identified Mr. and Mrs. Brown and Billy as a family now said no, they were not a family. "In the minds of three- to five year olds, when you say 'family,' they don't just think about a configuration, but an expectation of love and caring as well. When they talk about family, they talk about love. They talk about caring."

A family can be one mother, or one father, and children; it can be one parent, children, and a network of caring, dependable friends; it can be one child left, the last genetic bearer, grown now, with relatives and ancestors framed and on the wall. Do we wish to tell this man or woman, who has no living relatives left, that he or she has no family? A family exists specifically in the spirit and nowhere else.

Christmas Love Letters

ONE RECENT CHRISTMAS, MY FAMILY WROTE LOVE LISTS. My wife and I had been thinking about doing this since I had written a column about Linda Evangelist, of El Centro, California, who did not enjoy shopping.

Linda and the members of her family decided that, rather than buy each other presents, each would write love letters to the other family members, to be read aloud on Christmas morning. The love letters would list at least twenty-five reasons why the person receiving the letter was loved or valued.

Among the reasons her son Brad (then a teenager) gave for loving his dad: "You would bribe me to go get ice cream late at night after Mom went to bed."

Among the reasons her two sons gave for loving their mom: "You come up with weird ideas like this one."

Among the reasons the brothers gave for loving each other: "You rode me on your handlebars to school when I was in junior high," and "You were considerate enough to put your banana peels under the couch." And so on.

Christmas morning love lists have become a tradition in the Evangelist household—and in other homes, as well.

After that column appeared, I began to hear from people who had tried the idea. Among them was San Diegan Suzanne Hess, who, as I reported last year, sent me a rhyming love list that her thirteen-year-old son, Elliot, gave to her:

> *You are so nice, oh yes you are*
> *You're willing to drive me anywhere in that van you call a car*
> *Whenever I give you the same old story*
> *You always play along*
> *You were a hippie just like Cheech and Chong*
> *You take care of me when I'm ill*
> *You bring me a blanket when I get a chill*
> *You are unique and you will stay that way*
> *I am so serendipitous to be your son.*

The idea began to spread. Last year, at Christmas time, a talk-show host on Los Angles radio station KFI had read the entire column, over the air, about Linda Evangelist and her family's love lists. About that time I decided that my family had better get on board, too.

So this year, we sat down and wrote our own love lists. Actually, we splurged: We bought or made presents, and we wrote love lists, too. Obviously I can't report to you the total contents of our lists, and wouldn't anyway because some of the items would be too personal. As I write this, my wife and two sons and I haven't finished our lists, but here are a few items from my love lists.

Among the reasons I listed in my letter to my son, Jason: "You let me read you bedtime stories, even though you're twelve. You protect your brother even when he irritates you. You make a mess I wouldn't trade for anything. I can trust your word. You teach me about UFOs and comics. You work hard for a goal. You try to do what's right, even when it's hard to know what that is. You treat people with respect. You're dreamy and imaginative. You like me to watch *X-Files* with you with the lights turned off, and you tape it for me when I'm not home. You love your family. You sing to yourself . . . ."

Among others, I listed these reasons for valuing and loving my six-year-old, Matthew: "Every night when I tuck you in, you laugh at my joke: 'Can I take your glasses off so your nose can grow?' You like to fish even more than I do. Your enthusiasm for every moment. The way you snuggle. The way you laugh when I give you a belly beezle. You stand up for yourself. You love Rex the Wonder Dog, even when the rest of us have had it with his whining. You're full of love and life and laughter . . . ."

My list for Kathy, to whom I have been married for seventeen years, included: "You gave birth to Matthew and Jason. You care deeply about your patients at work. You're honorable in every part of your life. I trust you. You don't pick up my socks. You took care of my mother, and me, when she was dying. You go family camping when you'd rather get room service. You introduced me to the joys of room service. You read better books than I do. The scent of your clothes. The way you look when the covers are wrapped around your face. . . ."

I'm looking forward to giving these lists and to receiving mine. Perhaps your family could try it, too. It's just an idea; life's short.

Over the years, many people have adopted the tradition of Christmas Love Letters. One letter, a kind of parable, arrived from Victoria Modic. It told how her mother and younger sister, Regina, decided to try out the idea. "They met with much resistance from the rest of us," wrote Modic, "especially from my stoic dad, who couldn't understand why he needed to verbalize his feelings, since we obviously knew that he loved us. Finally, all family members agreed to do this, just to get mom and Regina off our backs. We compromised, however, on the number of reasons why we loved each other. Instead of twenty-five, we settled on five."

Christmas Day 1992 came. Modic's father had meticulously printed his list in his neat engineer's handwriting, and other family members had huddled in the dining room hurriedly compiling theirs. "When time came for the reading of the love lists, Dad was overcome with emotion and could not speak, so Regina and my husband, Frank, finished reading for him." Afterward, they agreed that this had been their best Christmas ever. Regina compiled the lists on the computer, and each family received a copy.

"On December 19, 1993, my father died suddenly of a massive heart attack," remembers Modic. "Since we were totally unprepared for this, we had no idea what to say for his eulogy. Then, Frank and Regina remembered the love lists and printed them out. Our cousin Kevin came down for the memorial Mass and delivered the eulogy. He read what each

of us had written about Dad, followed by what Dad had written about us. I'm sure that all who were present could not have failed to be touched by the love which existed between each of us in our relationship with him.

"The lesson to be learned through all of this," she added, "is that you never know when a loved one will die, and wouldn't it be wonderful if that person were told while still alive what he or she meant to you?"

The Man Who Reappeared

SOMETIMES, A PERSON CAN DISAPPEAR right before his own eyes.

During a recent trip to New York, I visited with an old friend. Actually, I had not known him that well. In high school, he had been smart and witty, one of those guys who thought he was too good for Kansas, who walked down the hall and looked right over you, or through you, as if you didn't exist.

Or at least, that's the way he remembers himself.

"The truth was, I was busy disappearing," he said. We were sitting in his office high above Manhattan. Today, he is a successful corporate lawyer.

"I've been disappearing all my life," he said. "Professionally, this works well for me. It's a way of not being in the room, of disconnecting from people. I can look them in the eye, nod appropriately and make noises, and yet I'm not really listening. I'm on to the next case."

But disappearing does not work well in a family.

"One day, during a ride up to the farm with my wife sitting next to me, I realized I was holding an imaginary conversation with her. She's sitting right there. Why am I not talking to her?"

Everybody does that, I said, some of the time.

"Sure they do," he said. "And anybody watching a couple doing that at, say, a restaurant, would think: There's an old married couple not talking to each other. But they're not dead; something is going on in their heads. They're probably having an imaginary conversation with somebody, maybe with each other."

As he discovered, disappearing from a child can be more difficult.

His first child, was born dead due to a syndrome that causes severe deformities in the skull and spine, and the absence of kidneys.

He did not disappear then. He was with his wife throughout the hideous night, as a blizzard howled outside the hospital window.

"You understand, I don't disappear during a crisis. That's one of the ways I have masked my everyday absences. And it's not that I don't spend time with my family. I do. That's why I'm a company lawyer instead of a member of a firm. The hours are predictable. I can be with my family."

But being with his family emotionally is different from being with them physically. He began to see that shortly after the birth of his daughter Judith.

During her first year, he became increasingly anxious and did not know why. He ascribed his nervousness to ordinary causes: job; physical health; turning forty. But slowly he realized that this tension was associated with his daughter.

"I was withdrawing from her. This withdrawing was happening every day. She would come toddling into the room and I would start listening to the radio, or I would start to walk into another room and my tension would build. I could feel it physically. It was a tingling sensation." He was disappearing in front of his daughter, just as, he remembered, his mother had done when he was a child.

He could not con or charm his daughter; he could not make a case, file a brief, slap her on the back to make it all right. He could see this in her eyes; he could see that she knew. And he knew that if he continued, then someday she would disappear, and he would lose her.

He decided to do something about his disappearing act.

The astonishing thing, he says, is that it took so long for a highly educated professional to figure out how to reappear. But this was a lifelong pattern, more ingrained than the usual parental distraction.

The changes were simple but very difficult. "When I found myself walking past my daughter as she approached me, I would say to myself, sometimes out loud, 'Stop. Turn around. Go back in there, and play with your daughter.'"

Feeling overwrought, he would walk back to her, get down on his hands and knees and play with her. He would look her in the eye and talk to her. He would focus on her as a person—as a person, not as a child. And his feelings of tension and unease would fade, at least temporarily.

He practiced, over and over. Sometimes he forgot; sometimes he began to slip away again, and then would snap himself back into focus. He began to see his own reflection return to his daughter's eyes.

"I had, of course, always been a nervous person. I had come to think of my never-ending tension as chronic background noise. I had assumed that this was just the way life was, and always would be, at least for me. Well, it's astonishing how much of that can go away.

First it went away when I was with my daughter, and I began to focus on my wife. 'Look at her, talk to her.' "

He even began to do this with people he worked with, and it transformed his relationships with them. "Simple things, nothing profound."

But, if not for his daughter, he said, he might have vanished completely.

The Garden

FOR DECADES, MY BROTHER AND I HAVE TENDED our relationship like an old and tangled garden. This has never been easy, but always necessary.

We share a code of language and loss, of symbols from long ago. We can recall together, as we can with no one else, the scent of the rooms and cellars and attics of our childhood. Sometimes, late at night and long-distance, we attempt to understand the equation of our parents. These conversations are our only living remnants of them. Perhaps we keep them alive this way, sometimes at our own risk.

In any case, our brotherhood is the longest relationship we will ever have; it is now forty years old, and if we live long enough, and tend it well, our relationship—our friendship—may last a half-century more.

Most of us will know our brothers and sisters longer than other friends or family members, including our parents, spouses, and children. And yet we do not know much about the dynamics of these bonds. Until recently, studies of the sibling relationship have been relatively scarce, yet interest in the sibling relationship is rising because of demographics; we are becoming a sibling society.

Most baby boomers have at least two siblings; at the same time, we have produced fewer children than preceding generations, and more of us will probably remain single as we age. We also live in a mobile, time-poor era when long-term friendships seem tenuous. So some social scientists believe that boomers, more than past generations, will turn to siblings for support and kinship. At least that's the theory.

Marian Sandmaier, author of *Original Kin: The Search for Connection Among Adult Sisters and Brothers*, writes: "The tie of time mingles with the tie of blood. A brother or sister shares, on average, fully half of our genes. One looks at a sibling and sees shards of self: the shape of a nose, the way the body is held, a mania for music, a to-the-death stubbornness. To have a brother or sister is to have someone who is, visibly and actually, part of oneself."

Genetic similarities are important, but shared history is also important, particularly for adoptive siblings. Who knows where nature ends and nurture begins? The mania my brother and I share is for fishing, for this was part of the healing adhesive for our fragile family together. We are still fragile.

Indeed, there is something innately ambivalent and difficult about the sibling bond. As Sandmaier writes, "the genetic glue ensures only a primitive loyalty." Primatologists report that conflict is more common, though not as intense, among primate siblings than among those not related. Siblings, it seems, like to fight.

The other night, after a long phone wrangle over what to do about our mother's house, I admitted to my brother: "I never yell at anyone like I yell at you. I seldom lose my temper. I don't understand it." It is as if brotherhood carries with it a license to vent. It is a dangerous license, for much could be lost.

Our occasional anger at each other is born of protectiveness, for we spent much of our childhood fearing for one another, and still do. These fears, along with jealousies and resentments, as well as bursts of love and recognition, are the fruits of our garden. But a garden, perhaps the best parts first, can wither.

Sibling feuds often spring up over the care of an aging parent, or, when the parents die, as the belongings of that other life are painfully split apart. We can find ourselves reeling backward into cartoonish roles that we thought we had left behind long ago.

To this day, my brother insists, half-jokingly, that I have more luck in fishing and in life, but I believe that I am more a fisher in theory than in practice; he is the one who, before he became a teacher, made a living on the sea. Perhaps, in subtle ways, both of us wish to keep the myth of our relative luck alive, however inaccurate.

Yet, what surprises me most about the gardens of brotherhood and sisterhood is their resilience. They do not spring from summer seeds, but from winter bulbs buried deep. Only about 3 percent of brothers and sisters formally cut the sibling bond. Despite the mixed emotions that many siblings feel toward each other, polls show that most Americans would like to see their siblings more often than the typical two or three times a year.

In an aging society, psychologists place more importance on nurturing the sibling relationship. Some promote "sibling therapy," similar to marriage therapy. It is true that we cannot "fix" a sibling, nor can a sibling fix us, but we can change our behavior; we can quit expecting our siblings to be like us; we can work to reshape the frozen images of one another. And though a death in the family can drive siblings apart, it can also end an estrangement. It can remind us of the fragility of memory and time.

Not every garden can grow, but some can be successfully weeded and watered with love and humor and a few new seeds. For my brother and me, it's time to do some planting. And then some fishing.

In the Pond

ONE DAY, MY SONS AND I DECIDED TO GO FISHING in the little pond near the local library. Rex the Wonder Dog threw himself in front of the van, so we opened the door and he got in. He made himself invisible, happily doing mathematical equations in his head or whatever dogs do when they're sitting in a motor vehicle.

We got to the pond and the dog said he preferred staying in the van. Jason helped Matthew bait his rod.

I got my belly boat out. A belly boat is a fancy inner tube with a sling underneath. You put on your waders and these huge frogman flippers that make it impossible to get into the tube without doing complicated pirouettes with your fishing rod whipping and your hat flying. Your sons watch you do this with perplexity and wonder.

My theory is that every day is Father's Day, including the days that you look like a fool. Especially the days you look like a fool.

Not long ago, my sons saw me fly. We were at the neighborhood park and they were jumping off a ledge, a bit timidly, and I said to them, "You can jump higher than that. Here, watch." I raced across the grass and leaped into the air and, at the very apogee of my trajectory, I stopped in midair, like Wile E. Coyote, and my feet started racing as I fell. I sat up on the grass and laughed. My sons were standing there with their mouths open. "I can still do this. I'm not that old," I said to myself. Applying every cell of my intelligence, I did it again.

This time I jumped higher. I waved at a passing jetliner that swerved to avoid me. And then I went into a dive. This time I heard something snap. I sat up. People were watching from across the park. One of my sons said, "Dad, don't do that again."

I chased after my sons and grabbed them and swung them around the park. They must have thought I had lost my mind, but it was probably just my youth, and the flexibility of my right shoulder. I suspect that my sons will replay this movie in their minds until their hair is grayer than mine. But I digress.

I fished for a while, kicking the flippers and gliding around the pond. My sons fished from shore. At the far end of the pond, three teenage boys were fishing and trying out profanity. It is difficult for teenagers to fish and be cool at the same time, but they were trying. Eventually, they left, woofing and hooting and heaving rocks into the pond to mark their exit.

I thought about how Jason will be a teenager soon.

Matthew was getting bored, so I offered to take him for a ride on the belly boat. He is at a stage when he is concerned about things like getting his feet wet. I told him I would try to keep his feet dry. Jason helped him onto the tube. He sat in my lap with his little feet up on the tube and I kicked off.

I looked back and saw a little loss in the older boy's eyes.

Matthew held my fly rod and the line drifted out

behind us as I trolled around the shore. We watched redwing blackbirds and listened to them rattle the rushes. Both of us were in heaven, or at least in one of its suburbs. After a while I kicked back to the shore and let the younger boy off.

"Dad, my butt is wet!"

"But your feet are dry."

Then, without calculating the ratio of weight to buoyancy, I asked Jason, "Would you like me to take you on the belly boat?"

His face lit up. He took off his shoes and socks and waded in and awkwardly sat down on the edge of the tube and leaned back in my arms. The tube rocked and wobbled and went lower in the water, but it stayed afloat.

We moved around the pond. I could tell by the shape of his cheek that he was smiling. The sun disappeared behind some trees. The pond darkened and grew mysterious. Moisture in the air made the trees at the far end of the pond fuse and shimmer.

"It's beautiful," Jason said in a quiet voice. "It looks like a jungle."

Meanwhile, back on the shore, Matthew was sitting on a stump; he was concerned, he explained later, that someone seeing his wet bottom would "think I peed in my pants."

Across the pond, I called to him, "How you doing Matthew?"

"Fine," he answered. When the rushes blocked my view of him, I called again. "Fine," he said. His voice was smaller now. "I heard something in the bushes."

"It's just the blackbirds," I called out.

Jason and I stayed out on the water and the minutes lengthened and seemed to slow almost to a halt. A street light shone through the branches. It looked like the moon. We drifted in the water together, and I thought to myself, will this be the last time I hold him in my lap?

By the time we got back to Matthew, he was swatting at his face and arms and crying a little bit, but still glued to that stump. A swarm of mosquitoes had come suddenly. I lurched from the belly boat and, like the Creature from the Black Lagoon, charged up the slope with flippers flapping and arms waving.

Matthew had convinced himself that a coyote was in the bushes, but he had sat as still and quiet as the moon. He had not wanted to appear foolish. We returned to the van, where the dog had worked out a new unified theory.

The next day the boys' mother counted their mosquito bites and entered them into the Louv Book of World Records: Jason, 72; Matthew 113. The younger boy was puffed up: he loved scoring higher than his older brother.

I felt a bit ashamed for not protecting them better, but foolishness and bug bites come with the territory.

In the years of my fatherhood, I have realized that when I am fathering I feel more like a man than at any other time in my life.

A Treasure Chest

THE OLD CHEST OF DRAWERS PROVED to be a treasure chest. It was a small piece of furniture, perhaps an old wash-stand, with three drawers. It sat in a storage unit for over a year, and when we bought a house with a garage, we moved it there, along with stacks of boxes filled with the remains of my mother's life. As everyone must do some-day, my wife and I sorted out the heirlooms. But for the longest time I could not bear to disturb the chest, as if it slept.

This chest had held my mother's art supplies. She made her living as a greeting card artist. She began work-ing in Kansas City, at age sixteen, for Hallmark Cards, and over the years became known as one of the best freelance greeting card artists.

I grew up watching her work. I would stand next to her art table and watch her hand move the brush ex-pertly across the paper and then move to the right, to the chest, where she would dip it into blotches of paint or stir the brush loudly in an old fruit jar of water.

The paints and an airbrush and her heavy tape dis-penser and her scissors were kept there. From time to time, the tape or the scissors would disappear, and she would call out irritated to her two boys to bring them back. But she never banned us from her desk. The squares of blotter paper she cut out were just right for our draw-ings, and our drawings littered the floor below the table.

Over the years, she covered the chest with layers of spilled paint and ink and tattooed it with cigarette burns. She was always leaving her cigarettes burning.

A couple of weekends ago, I decided that the time had come to go through the chest and refinish it and give it a new life. I sat on the garage floor and sorted through the treasures she had stashed there over the years. They were jumbled in time and space.

Among them:

A list of Ghostbuster action figures, written by my son, Jason, when he was in kindergarten.

A wallet-sized photograph of my father when he was in his twenties, very solemn and grown up.

An envelope postmarked September 1, 1931, 7 P.M., with a grocery list written on it by my grandmother, preparing for my mother's seventh birthday party. "Large dice for Pauline. Roller skates, $1.17. 15 gifts, 5 cents ea., two cakes 50 cents." Fifteen names were written on the envelope: Betty, Patsy, Bertha, Carl, Pet, Stanley.

A story recounting a family fish tale: "The gar the kid and the kid's brother. A true story by Jason F. Louv. Once upon a time there was a kid his name was Rich and his brother and once they were floating in the water behind the bote and the parents in the bote caught a gar it struggled they were scared they throt it off the bote the end."

A genealogy, in my mother's handwriting, of her family: "All were farmers except for one Herr, who was a lawyer. Only interesting fact was about Thomas Mifflin. He was a Brigadier General in the Revolutionary War. . . ." The Streeters, she wrote, came "across the U.S. to Nebraska in covered wagons."

Bottles of ink, squeezed tubes of paint. An address book from the '50s. A letter my mother, as a little girl, wrote on lined notebook paper in tortured, just-learned cursive: "Dear Arthur. How are you? I am fine. I love you very much. Where were you Saturday and Sunday. I wanted to play with you. This is why I wanted to because I didn't have anybody to play with. Alice was gone to the lake and Marjorie went to her Grandmother's house to stay one month. And now I have no one to play with. Will you please tell me what grade you are in, Arthur. For the first time in school I am using ink . . . ."

Blotter paper, tracing paper, nozzles to an airbrush.

Her husband's—my father's—death certificate.

A 1933 letter from my grandfather, whom I never met because he died when my mother was nine years old. He was a supervisor for Kansas City Southern railroad. The letter is to someone named Charlie: "Business is picking up a little and people are more hopeful—the railroads are doing some better especially in freight traffic—we're all wondering what will result from Roosevelt's proposed rail central plan . . . ."

An old column of mine.

Stacks of roughs for my mother's greeting cards. Correspondence from the greeting card publishers. Deadlines set. Deadlines met. Lists of cards to do: "Madonna child, Lambs, Angel, Christ, Angel Head & Wings, Blue Sky, Profile Child, Santa on skis . . . ."

A hand-drawn card from Jason to her: "We were meaning to tell you . . . you're a great grandma. Merry Christmas."

I finished sorting the contents of the chest and packed them into cardboard boxes, then dragged the chest to the middle of the garage. A neighbor came by. "That's very old," he said, inspecting the unfamiliar tongue and groove joints. It had originally been in my grandmother's house in Independence, Missouri. I spent the next six hours bent over the chest, leaning into the grain.

Perhaps it was the noise from the electric sander, or the repetitive motion, or the concentration, but as I wore away the years, I heard my mother's voice. We talked all afternoon.

"Richy, your drawing is wonderful." A deep red stain was fading. "Have you seen my tape?" I heard her laughing. I heard her swear. "I don't like antiques. I like contemporary." She told me about my grandmother, and about my grandfather. The green lifted. "See what your brother's up to." Cigarette burns vanished. "Do it right or don't do it at all." I heard a sound like the ringing of a bell. It was my mother's brush in the old fruit jar.

Year after year, decade after decade, perhaps even a century, lifted from the wood.

The sawdust began to smell fresher, newer, expectant.

I stood back and looked at the chest. A few of my mother's marks remained. I thought: Perhaps I have gone too far; I should have left more of her there.

I heard her say she was pleased.

The chest, now quiet, is in our family room.

It remains unfinished.

When I consider my wife, I see the way her mouth moves when she whispers, the way her hair is feathered at the nape of her neck; and I hear her stories and feel her touch. And when I consider my marriage, no matter where I am, I enter a different place, a kind of shelter, a white room.

I do not know what will happen to this room if one of us should die, but I do know that this room exists now. When we lie curled together like strands of DNA, we know, somehow, that this is where we were meant to be. Sometimes beyond the room we can hear voices calling, but the voices are only the wind, air and time. A man and woman who are truly married, by license or not, understand that they live in the room in which they belong. The understanding of this room is what gives fidelity its meaning.

My wife and I are the conduit through which other souls pass. These souls are in this room with us. From her side and all the sides that made her, come the precisions of Switzerland, the passions of Sicily, the close voices of her father and mother and the distant sadness of her grandparents, immigrants in time who worked in kitchens and in factories and called to one another or did not call at all. And from my side comes the sharp fatalism of Truman's country, the shadows of prairie schooners, and some madness, and the vanity of itinerant artists, and, long before that, the veined hands of silk farmers. And through both of us come the pain and the hope of Cro Magnon and perhaps Neanderthal, and round-eyed *lemurs watching. Before that, there was only wind, and desire.*

All of this and more comes with us to this room, and out of our marriage it will move on, and we will move with it through our children, into other rooms. Our voices and longings will join those of future Swedes or Africans or Venetian colonists, and their stories will become ours, and ours theirs.

When I look carefully at my wife, I see her true beauty, both frightening and comforting. She has come to me, and I to her, to give the past a future and the future a past, to live for a while in this room.

The Strand
of Friendship

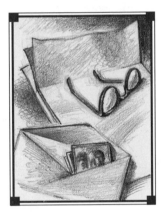

Friendship! mysterious cement of the soul!
Sweetener of life! and solder of society!
—Robert Blair, 1699–1747

The SLOP House

A FEW MORNINGS AGO, I WAS TALKING with a man who is in his eighties. I had heard that he had experienced a recent sadness in his life, and I told him that I hoped the sadness would pass. But my attempt to comfort him was, perhaps, gratuitous. He had lost his last best friend that week and such pain does not pass; it only fades, if there is time for the fading.

"If I was not so long-lived, I would not be suffering like this," he said. All of his fame and achievements and honors seemed to mean nothing that morning; they were like rumors, they were not real. What was real was that his last best friend was gone.

What defines a friend? A friend, it seems to me, is someone you can call when you have nothing to say. But a good friend is more than that. Friendship, by nature, is mysterious, and these days, undervalued. Even through the first half of this century, friendship seemed much more highly prized than it does today. The collected letters of, say, Eleanor Roosevelt or John Steinbeck reveal complex friendships that lasted and grew for decades, surviving the coming and going of wives and husbands, war and peace, sin and salvation. Perhaps the value placed on friendship then seems so much higher to us now because friendship then was better recorded. People wrote letters, and kept them in shoeboxes filled with time.

If you believe what you see on television, friendship

is making a comeback. The newest season is filled with knockoffs of sit-coms based on friendship. The locales of these programs are interesting. Not so long ago, many sit-coms were based on the premise that the workplace is a surrogate family and where we find our friends. Now the sit-coms are returning friendship to the living room, the apartment complex, the neighborhood.

Probably unintentionally, the producers are on to something. While it is still possible for friendship to flourish in the workplace, an increasingly competitive work environment can prevent or twist the strand of friendship. "I trust people less at work than I used to, so it's tougher to make and keep friends that way," says a friend of mine. "On the other hand, when I meet someone I like, I spend more time making friends if I know that this person can help my career." That's a lousy thing to admit, he says, "but it's true."

Another friend, Dave, who grew up in the late 1940s and 1950s in the rural Midwest, remembers when "work was work and life was life, but now life is all work." And he remembers how "distance was such a barrier that people were forced to know each other, for better or worse. People couldn't afford to pay a roofer, or the roofer was too far away. So fixing a roof was something you asked a friend or neighbor to help you with."

Mobility doesn't help. More than two-thirds of Americans have lost touch with a close friend, usually because someone moved, according to a 1992 Gallup poll. The most mobile groups, college graduates and baby boomers, are also the people who have lost the most friends. (The title of a 1972 novel by Larry McMurty comes to mind: *All My Friends are Going to Be Strangers*.) Even if we stay in the same state, we live an increasingly trans-regional lifestyle. Daily, we bounce from neighborhood to business district, to our children's schools, to the gym. The process weakens one of the glues of friendship, a shared sense of place. The trans-regional lifestyle can be especially painful for children, so often bused to schools or child care far from their neighborhoods.

So we hire professionals. During a trip to Russia, I was informed, by a rather smug Russian: "In Russia we have friends, in America you have psychiatrists." I had to admit there was some truth to this.

Still, a few trends suggest that friendship may, in fact, have a chance. According to recent census reports, American mobility has slowed a bit. Like it or not, as the nuclear family has given way to more complex networks of support, friends have become more important; for example, single parents come to depend more on their friends, especially other single parents. And as friendship in the workplace grows tenuous, Americans may be forced to search for it in more traditional venues: neighborhoods, churches, old-fashioned service, and social groups.

My friend Dave rejected the corporate life and now works at home as a designer in Southern California. To counter his isolation, he joined a Norwegian chorus, which performs at nursing homes and churches. This chorus has reconnected him to his Midwestern roots. "I find friendship in this group," he says. "Many of the men in it are very different from me, but I find that this is true of friendship in general. My friends are very diverse." Friendship is based on chemistry and trust, he adds, and why it happens or why it rises and falls, and rises again, is a mystery, like a fine piece of music. Here is his definition of friendship: "A friend accepts you for who you are, but expects you to be all you can be."

There is another argument for friendship's return. We're growing older, and friendship is good for our health. In recent years, researchers have found that a good friendship network can fight off depression and despair and can improve physical well-being. Stanford researchers have shown that terminally ill breast cancer patients who participate in support groups live twice as long as those who do not join a group. Will health-conscious boomers begin to turn to friendship as the latest holistic cure?

If government turns its back on the elderly, will we turn to each other for support? Maybe the lucky and the popular will. My friend Liz tells me her plans for old age. When she was in her early thirties, living in Illinois, Liz and four friends began to call their friendship network "the Digits." The Digits, she explains, were acting out their "latent sorority urges." One night, during a long talk about the fragility of family and the passing of years, the Digits came up with the idea of the "SLOP House." "That stands for sex and laughter for old people," she explains to me with a smile and a glint in her eye.

"The idea is to buy a piece of property, maybe in upstate New York or the Midwest, near a small college. We'll move there when we're of retirement age. We'll build the house ourselves. We imagine it will have a huge wrap around porch, a Japanese bath, a big kitchen, and each of us will have a private area. We want this house to have separate outbuildings from which we can operate small businesses, including perhaps a small publishing company."

"The SLOP Press?" I ask. She laughs.

"We could pursue other businesses: weaving, selling beautiful, handmade things. We could host musical events there, a lecture series, writers could come and read. It will be a house where young people will want to come—because we are so terribly interesting."

She cocks an eyebrow and adds, "We have agreed that anyone we dated or married would have to believe in this program. We'll come there with or without our husbands or mates."

The years have passed and the Digits have gone their separate ways, some into marriage, others out of state. But they have stayed in touch, and they continue to talk about the idea of a friendship stop at the end of life. The actuarial tables reveal that these women will probably outlive their husbands, so it's good to know the SLOP House awaits. "None of us can imagine ourselves moving to a retirement community. We want to be with our friends. Support each other, be with each other, make the final step with each other. I'll keep you posted."

I believe that the souls of women flatten and anchor themselves in times of adversity, lay in for the stay. I've heard that when elephants are attacked they often run, not away, but toward each other. Perhaps it is because they are a matriarchal society.

—novelist Elizabeth Berg, Talk Before Sleep

The Greatest Gift is Your Honest Self

FRED ROGERS ENTERS A NOISY HOTEL LOBBY, taking pictures of the people who have come to meet him. You realize that you have lowered the volume of your voice.

I look down at my son, Matthew, who has recently turned six. Normally ebullient and outgoing, Matthew is rigid with tension, and I notice that his upper lip is quivering. Rogers smiles and shakes his hand and, before long, interrupts his conversation with the two adults and begins to talk directly to Matthew.

Noticing that Matthew has pulled a book about rocks out of his little backpack, Mister Rogers tells Matthew that he loves rocks, too, and that he owns a lapidary machine, which he keeps in an outbuilding on his property because of its constant whirring.

Matthew's eyes widen. His own birthday present was a lapidary machine, which right now is in our house rolling and polishing some of the billion or so rocks that he has collected.

Rogers asks Matthew to show him his book and now, together, they whisper the secrets of stone. In town to inaugurate a library program of his, Fred Rogers has pushed aside the business at hand to focus on one child. I wonder: How many thousands of other children has Mister Rogers connected with in this way? For most people, such continual expectation of attentiveness would wear thin. I ask him about this.

"I think if I were playing a part, that would really bother me. I don't play the part of Mister Rogers. I *am* Mister Rogers," he says. "One of the most important gifts you can give anybody, is the gift of your honest self."

To his satirists, his cardigan sweater and soft voice are more bizarre than any clown wig or polka-dot suit; he is that rarest of television creatures: real. I ask how he feels about the frequent impersonations by comedians, most especially Eddie Murphy's scalding sendup on *Saturday Night Live: Mister Robinson's Neighborhood* ("Children, can you say pipe bomb?").

The satire bothered Rogers at first, he says, but over time he has become convinced that most of it is done with affection. Not long ago, he met Murphy, who burst out of his office, arms spread, grinning, and said, "It's the real Mister Rogers!" Mister Rogers spread his arms and said, "It's the real Mister Robinson!"

Other impersonations have not been so affectionate. Legal action was used to stop the Ku Klux Klan in a Midwestern town from passing out slips of paper in schoolyards encouraging children to call a telephone number: a voice sounding like Mister Rogers answered with racial and religious hate messages.

Later, Rogers tells me he thinks some of the more vitriolic satire is done by people with a deep longing for a gentle father in their lives. Indeed, as the host of *Mister Rogers' Neighborhood* on PBS for twenty-five years, he has been a strong male presence in the lives of many children. A friend.

Rogers, now sixty-five, recalls his inspiration to enter

the medium. "It was Easter, 1951, and I saw people on television throwing pies at each other and I thought, I want to work in that medium. To think what I would see now ... it breaks my heart."

He is deeply troubled by the violence and quickening pace of children's entertainment. He says he does not watch much television himself. He has never seen *Beavis and Butt-Head*, the 1990s cartoon satire of suburban TV-dominated adolescence. When children go to the refrigerator, he says, they assume that what the adults in the family have put in it is not poisonous. Children think of television in the same way.

Despite his anger at TV violence, he stops short of any political statement, any endorsement of proposed legislation to curb the violence, but he does not reject the idea. "There is so much we can do that has nothing to do with censorship. I know many people in the industry with basically good motives. They're going to have to limit themselves, even if it means not making quite so many millions of dollars."

He pauses.

"Isn't it amazing how much human beings are able to take? I wonder what the breaking point is. But I always look for the faithful remnant. You think that everything is lost and nobody believes in anything that is healthy anymore and all of a sudden you find this faithful remnant of hope. It's like my mother said, always look for the helpers. At the edge of any disaster, you will find them."

Remembering that Rogers is an ordained minister (and this explains something about his essential nature; he is more spiritual friend than activist), I mentioned to him that Matthew had asked me a theological question the other day, for which I did not have a good answer.

"What was it?" Rogers asked.

"Matthew said, 'Dad, I've been wondering about something. Is God married to Mother Nature or are they just good friends?' "

I had involuntarily laughed when my son said this. Like most parents, I don't always take my children's pronouncements as seriously as I should, and my reactions have, in the past, understandably angered Matthew.

Mister Rogers does not laugh.

"That's a very interesting question, Matthew." He thinks about it for a long moment. "Your mom and your dad are married and they've had two fine boys, and they're mighty important to those two boys, and I think that's one way we get to know what God and Nature are like, by having a mom and a dad who love us." Maybe the statement isn't exactly politically correct (what about single parents?), but the answer seems to work for Matthew, who nods.

Later, as everyone stands to leave, Mister Rogers walks over and sits next to my son. "Will you let me know, as time goes by, what answer you find to your question?" he asks gently. He is reopening the door to the question, encouraging Matthew to have the last word.

That is what a real friend does.

Friendship is a sheltering tree.
                    –Samuel Taylor Coleridge, 1772–1834

What Our Pets Teach Us

FOR YEARS, I HAVE SECRETLY BELIEVED that the dog I grew up with was something of a moral teacher in our family. Admitting this belief, I invite all sorts of critiques from those who, for religious or scientific reasons, object to attributing humanlike behavior to nonhuman animals. So be it. I'll bet you had such a special friend, too.

Not long ago, I asked an animal behavioralist if dogs can be moral teachers to children. (I suppose they can be moral teachers to adults, too, but children and dogs, like Elwood P. Dowd and Harvey, can be especially attuned.) This particular animal behaviorist also earned a doctorate in the psychology of human behavior, and he is an expert on pet therapy for children.

Pets, he said, are often moral teachers, though that is not their intent. For example, pets teach children about death. "The death of a dog or cat can be the single most profound loss a human being can experience. Some people don't want to accept the fact that an animal can mean as much, or more, to a human being as another member of the family. But it can. Children learn about dying; they can afford this price more than they can the loss of a parent."

A dog can teach a child about unqualified love. A child may have trouble reading even a loving parent, but a dog is always straightforward. "Dogs do not deceive well. They don't lie. The most they do is misunderstand."

Unfortunately, dogs may be the only source of unqualified, unearned affection that some children ever have.

Dogs also teach about the difference between essence and behavior, about human forgiveness. "When my kid does something wrong and I explode, it's hard for the child to realize I love him," he says. "But when my child sees me punishing the dog, and then twenty minutes later giving it treats, loving it, paying its vet bill, my child realizes that the dog's behavior is bad, but the dog is still good." On the other hand, when parents use corporal punishment on a dog, "it teaches a child that swatting a butt is a good idea." That is a lesson more children could do without.

I pointed out that his examples had focused more on parental behavior than pet behavior. I wanted to return to my original question. "Let me ask you about Banner," I said to the animal behavioralist.

Banner was two when he came, and eleven when he died, and in between he was my best friend, and, I believed, my teacher.

Now I will admit right off that the memory of a child is imaginative. Banner was a collie in the era of Lassie and Jeff. And, as a child, I devoured the books of Albert Payson Terhune, who wrote "Lad: A Dog." So these undoubtedly influenced my expectations and perhaps my memory.

Still, I do remember these things. Banner, whose nose was scarred deeply by the time he died, would never fight a smaller dog; sometimes he would protect the smaller dogs of the neighborhood. Grumping about it the whole time, he would walk out of the basement each morning with the cat between his legs, protected. I watched him shoot up the street and catch the neighborhood's meanest dog in midair as it attacked a neighbor, who was holding her small dog in her arms. Banner would pull my brother by the diapers from the street. He would sit on us when we threw rocks. When we were up to no good he would sometimes go home, but he would always come back.

I spent centuries, it seemed, in the woods with Banner. Once, when I was about eight, I fell through the ice of the creek. Up to my waist, I tried to climb the steep and snowy bank but slipped back. Banner left. He came back. I remember him at one end of a fallen branch, tugging, and I remember getting out of the creek that way.

I tell you this with some embarrassment, knowing the trickery of memory. I don't know if any of this happened exactly the way I remember.

Children romanticize their pets, project all kinds of behavior onto them, the behavioralist said. Dogs often tend to fight the largest dog available, he explained. They are doing what dogs do; they do not think about championing the oppressed. The branch was probably there all along, and Banner was probably only playing tug-of-war. "Your interpretation was the lesson," he said. "Perhaps you unconsciously aggrandized yourself by seeing his behavior as heroic. But who taught him to tug on the stick—an act that may have unintentionally saved your life? Probably you taught him that."

The behavioralist's rationality is appealing, but so is mystery.

Buddhists, I am told, believe that a teacher or priest who fails to live a good life can find himself demoted in the next life. He can find himself in the form of a dog, still with the urge to teach.

One dark morning I awakened to the sound of my mother crying. I was convinced that something had happened to my father. I ran down the stairs and out to the porch to find Banner, carried from the road by my father, was lying there cold and stiff. I cried, but the crying was fake—I was relieved that my father still lived. For a long time, I felt guilty for that secret fakery. So Banner taught me about the confusion and untidiness of death.

Sometimes when I return to Kansas City, I walk back behind the old house where there is a depression in the ground. Here lies my friend. I wonder where he really is.

Two Rivers

We drove northeast from Espanola, where my farmer/woodworker/trout-fisher friend Nick lives with his family. We drove through the thin curtains of rain that drift across the flatlands between the mountains of New Mexico.

In February, my wife had called Nick, whom I have not seen in five years, and arranged a forced vacation for me. There is a Turkish proverb that a day spent fishing is not subtracted from your life. There should be another proverb that says that two fathers fly-fishing will talk about three things (in addition to the drift of the stream and other minutiae): sex, death, and raising kids.

Whenever Nick and I get together, we continue our conversation in midstream, as we did this time, standing in the Cimmaron. Actually, we did not talk much about sex. Since I last saw him, Nick has gone from being a dour Marxist to a Christian literalist. (Neither dour Marxists nor Christian literalists talk much about sex, at least not directly.) So we talked a lot about our kids, not in the oblique way that men so often do, but directly.

Nick and I are different in our fathering; he is an undoubting nineteenth century father; I am a doubting twentieth century dad. He believes, for example, in corporal punishment. I do not. We talked about this on the river.

"I figure discipline is like the arms race," I said, as I

55

tied on a sinking nymph. The spring water was high and murky, and not good for dry flies. Nick, being Calvinistic, tied on a floating caddis. I shoved my glasses up on my forehead so that I could see the fly. The last time Nick and I fished, I did not have this problem.

"If your child believes that a time-out is the ultimate punishment," I continued, "he will generally push and test until he reaches that limit. But once you've spanked a child, that becomes the ultimate punishment and you will have to use that punishment from then on."

"Well, that makes some sense," he said.

Nick was just upstream, working a pool. He was wearing torn and stained jeans and very old tennis shoes. I was wearing my new neoprene waders that protect me from the painfully cold mountain water. This is another way we are different. Nick has led a more spartan life, to say the least.

He did not attempt to defend spanking, just as I did not attempt to defend time-outs. Some child-rearing experts do not like spanking or time-outs.

"What about the schools in California," Nick asked. "Don't the teachers use corporal punishment?"

"No. I think it's against the law."

"You're kidding. How do the teachers keep control?"

I said I wasn't sure.

"Maybe that's why California is out of control," he said.

I was not sure how to respond.

This is where our river branches: I believe that fish should be caught and released; Nick believes they should be caught and eaten, and anything short of that is torture to the fish. I believe that the world is harsh and violent enough as it is, and I do not have to impose any more of that on my children. In fact, part of my job as a parent is to protect my sons, as long as I can, from the brutality of the world. He believes that violence is inevitable, that suffering is redemptive, and that a father must teach his children about the harshness of life by exposing them to that harshness.

When Nick's children were small and he and his family still lived on their farm down a dirt road in a valley of adobes and cottonwoods and chiles, his daughter came home one day to find her favorite goat (not a pet, really, but one that followed her around) skinned, gutted, and strung up in the barn. This was a time when Nick's family was short on shoes, and the meat they ate was meat that Nick butchered or shot with his gun. It was a terrible moment for his daughter.

Nick insists he has no regrets, but he still talks about it. "She was hurt, but she knew from that moment on, and will for the rest of her life, where the meat that she eats comes from, and that meat is not born plastic-wrapped." This is not the kind of experience I would have wanted for my children, but I have had a different life.

Nick is among the hardest workers and thinkers I have known; he believes deeply in the value of using his hands to grow and make what his family needs. He pores over the classics: Plato and Aristotle and Kierkegaard and, of course, the Bible. His has been an essentially nineteenth century education, and he has passed this on to his children, and they have thrived, becoming scholars and leaders.

Nick's children are leaving the nest now. The evidence is in: His children are wonderful people, self-confident, self-disciplined, independent, and not afraid of anyone, including their father. However differently he and I do our fathering, I admire how he and his strong and nurturing wife have succeeded in this life. Evidence in my life is in, too, but not all of it; we'll see how I do with my sons' adolescence.

Nick and I have moved down the stream, and, as Nick fishes, he talks with deep love and admiration for his children, not only as his progeny but as people. Here is where the branches of our river come together again and form a long, smooth pool, where the trout grow fat and strong, and surface gently, making rings in the darkening water.

Why does age make such a difference to friendship? The year that divides a second grader and third grader, or even an eighth or ninth grader, is enough to prevent friendship, at least in a school hallway in the presence of peers. Twenty five year olds are unlikely to hang out with seventeen year olds, often with good reason. This inverse relationship between age and friendship seems to intensify over time. But there are always exceptions. And as we enter mid-life these distinctions begin to fade. Now that I am in my forties, I realize that my friendship web has widened. These days, I have friends who are years, and sometimes decades, older or younger than I. This is part of the grace of aging.

Unfolding Friendship

A FEW YEARS AGO, WHEN MY OLDER SON AND I went to a baseball game, the car steamed over. As we sat in the dark waiting for the engine to cool, a carload of teenaged boys went by, hooting and squawking and waving their limbs from the windows.

"Why do teenagers dress so funny and act so stupid?" asked Jason. He was nine then. "Because they're separating from their parents," I said. "They want to be different from their parents."

Jason was silent. I glanced over. I could see his silhouette in the light of passing cars. Finally he said, "I don't want to separate. I love you and Mom." I explained what I had meant: that teenagers must become their own people, but they do not have to separate completely from their families. Perhaps I was trying to convince myself. Jason seemed satisfied with my explanation. We sat there a while longer, watching the lights of the cars.

Now we are entering those years together. I need more convincing. For decades, parents have thought that the parent-teen conflict was natural, according to Eleanor Maccoby, professor of psychology at Stanford University. "The conventional wisdom was that the kids should fight to be free from their parents, and their parents should give up control as gracefully as possible, and that if the right values had not been instilled in the child by this age, it was too late." But current research is more hopeful.

Maccoby says adolescents should be allowed to act more independently, but parents and teens should not disengage. "Rather, they should move toward the kind of relationship that adults who are close have with one another." Maccoby's description of this relationship is fascinating. Adults who are close—friends or family—are never totally autonomous. They maintain their relationship within a binding network, agree to coordinate activities, negotiate the division of labor, and try to show up on time for meetings with each other. This is the relationship that parents and adolescents need to move toward, rather than total independence.

This, it seems to me, is a fascinating way to view the transition of adolescence—the transformation of parent as well as child.

Not long ago, I was invited to meet with a group of psychologists that convenes for breakfast once a month to share their personal concerns, as men and as fathers. I took advantage of the invitation to ask them for some tips on raising an adolescent.

In particular, I wanted to know: Is the struggle between fathers and teenage sons inevitable? "I think an emotionally violent conflict is avoidable," said one psychologist. Others said that the conflict is necessary but can be softened. Until eleven or twelve, children rely primarily on their parents for their moral and intellectual guideposts, but then they begin to reach beyond their parents.

The psychologists advised: You're no longer the only man in his life; adolescence is a time when he must reach out to other men for mentoring, learning, growth. A father can feel a mixture of pride and pain at this inevitable separation. It helps to know that you're not being permanently replaced and that your son's reaching out is part of his development. Accept your son's challenge, the psychologists recommended. It's your child's destiny to compete with you, to question your rules, even your feelings. As one psychologist put it with a gentle laugh, "The moment of truth comes when you realize your son has more testosterone than you do. Your response to this challenge can make or break the relationship." Reject it, and you and your child are in trouble; accept it, and you can help your son win a few. Stay engaged: Compete, but not to win at any cost.

In the best father-son relationships, one of the psychologists said, there is "a certain playfulness, a wrestling battle." When your son does win, rejoice in his growth. Be friends, as best you can. The nature of the conflict between a father and an adolescent son is determined by the quality of their friendship.

Sometimes, of course, the father and son love each other, but the relationship disintegrates anyway. Have faith. Healing can come many years later. One man remembered something his father had said to him one day: "I never got the grade-point average that you do. I'm proud of you." Whatever else this father and son said to each other over several rocky years, that sentence survived.

One more thing: Do not to expect long, mano-a-mano talks, they advised. Particularly at twelve or thirteen, young people are struggling with hormonal changes; they're overloaded, flooded and usually not able to verbalize, at least not to parents, their inner turmoil. But action helps. Go fishing. Go to the gym together. One psychologist put it this way: Build an "action relationship."

I came away from this conversation feeling better about my relationship with my sons and about the future. Like every other stage of a child's growth, adolescence marks the end of something, but it also marks a beginning.

These days, Jason is more circumspect. In our house we seldom talk at length, but there is something about walking or riding bikes together that helps him emerge from the place to which teenagers go, and helps me escape some of the confines of fatherhood. As we walk, I listen to him describe his world—of comics and, now, increasingly of music and film. These worlds are metaphors for his feelings. During these walks I sometimes find myself forgetting that I am his father; and my discomfort at his growth is quieted. As we walk, he becomes more comfortable with the person he is becoming. Between us, during these moments, fragile new strands are forming. I am listening. I am being his friend. We are walking side by side.

No one is wise enough by himself.

—Titus Maccius Plautus

An Old Woman of the Prairie

UNTIL RECENTLY, I WASN'T SURE IF Mrs. Hollembeak was still alive, or if my memory had made her bigger than reality. I first met Mrs. Hollembeak twenty-two years ago when I worked for a summer on the newspaper in Arkansas City, a hard-edged little town on the Oklahoma border. I was nineteen and knew no one in the town beyond the paper's staff. My high school history teacher in Kansas City, Gerald Hollembeak, had suggested I look up his mother.

So I did. In June 1968, I introduced myself to her. Her husband had died in 1959, and since then she had lived alone. Every few evenings we would talk about politics, about religion, about what we came to call "the ache," the painful pleasure of being alive.

As I came to know and admire her, I was moved by her wisdom—how she conserved what was valuable, appreciated what was small, needed little, but had a mind as broad as the prairie itself. She had written poetry all of her life, scribbled on scraps of paper. When I returned to college, after my summer in Ark City, sometimes a poem or two would arrive in the mail.

But I had not seen her since that summer.

So now, at dusk, I walked up the sidewalk to her three-room house. She opened the screen door. Her face, small and pixieish, creased into a broad smile. I sat on the same couch that I had in the summer of 1968. She sat in the same rocking chair. She was now ninety-one years old, but it was hard to think of her as old, or young, or any age. We picked up the conversation seemingly in mid-sentence.

I mentioned some of my memories of her, how she would play Beatles records, sitting there alone in her Spartan little cottage. And how, in 1968, she had read passages from black radical Eldridge Cleaver's book, *Soul on Ice,* to her adult Sunday school class, without mentioning the author's name. She smiled. "Cleaver was an uncouth man, but there was something in what he wrote. If I told them who wrote it, that would have set them back a bit."

She walked into the next room and brought out a family scrapbook that her sons had assembled for her. It included newspaper clippings from 1899, on the day she was born: an interview with Frank James in which he denied that he and his brother, Jesse, rode with Quantrill in his pre-Civil War raid on Lawrence, Kansas. Another article reported public fear of a possible Indian uprising.

She was raised on the prairie miles from other settlements. She grew up before radio, and read by a kerosene lamp. Her family butchered their own hogs and canned the meat on the kitchen wood stove. "When I was a girl, women didn't have the right to vote. Can you believe it? I was a suffragette!" She remembers Teddy Roosevelt running for president as a Bull Mooser; news of who won presidential races would often arrive days after the election.

Some nights, her mother would put out bowls of apples for the kids to peel and eat, and perhaps a bowl of popcorn. On some evenings, neighbors would gather. Her bearded father and the other men would go to the next room and chew tobacco and talk politics. They called themselves "the men's club." In another room, the women would do kitchen work or sew and talk, too. "I had big ears, so I was well informed."

Her mother died when she was eleven. She remembers her father building the long box with his own hands, and seeing her mother's body in bed. She remembers vividly how the neighbors came for a final visit, how the women sewed the burial dress and gently slipped it on. And she remembers how her father held her mother in his arms and laid her down in her coffin. "All of this was done with loving hands."

She didn't fly in an airplane until she was in her late seventies. The one modern technological device she loves is the microwave oven. She just can't get over it. "It's truly a miracle."

After her husband died, she felt no need for another man. She liked men fine as friends, she said, but "why would I need another marriage if I was fulfilled in the first?" She has remained alone for thirty-one years. She is amazed and awed and touched, even now—perhaps especially now—at the smallest things. "My sons say I can get more out of watching a butterfly than anybody they know. Lately, I've been drinking up autumn."

One recent evening she was sitting out on the porch watching the bats dip and shoot. Silently, behind her, someone cut a hole in her screen, climbed into her house and took sixteen dollars out of her purse. She felt enraged and violated. She began to lock her door for the first time in her life. Not long after the theft, she wrote a poem about it, and at the end of the poem she forgave the thieves, teenagers she thinks she knows. She remembers seeing one of them across the road, standing in the darkness, watching.

What she finds most difficult to accept about the theft is the lack of self-worth a young person must feel to victimize someone in her nineties. She sat forward quickly and said, "You like yourself, don't you?"

"Sure. Most of the time."

She sat back, narrowed her eyes, then smiled.

She said she doesn't attend church anymore. Her ideas about religion have changed over the years. She has gently moved away from dogma. She is uncomfortable with some of the narrow-mindedness she sees among many religious people today, particularly the young ones.

"But I do feel a presence. More each day."

She prays often, but asks for nothing. She considers praying a way of sharing, not asking. She thinks of it as a release—like her poetry.

Most days, she walks a mile to the grocery store. When she returns, she says, "Thank you, Lord, for helping me with that walk." When she takes down her hair to wash it in the bathtub, she gets dizzy. She'll sit for a moment on the edge of the bathtub, and say, "Thank you for helping me with my hair." She says these prayers out loud. "Maybe because I've lived alone for so long."

I asked her if she believed in an afterlife.

"Don't need one," she said, quickly. "I've had a long,

full life. One is enough." Still, she sometimes wonders if there is an afterlife—not for her, but for those who die young, like the baby she buried so many decades ago, or the son she lost to World War II.

Suddenly I realized it was 12:30 A.M. Just as in the summer of 1968, the time had gone by without notice. I stood to leave. She stood, too, with her arm across the back of the rocker.

"Mrs. Hollembeak," I asked, "what do you think this presence will do with you when you die? Will you become part of it?"

She thought about this for a moment, and then uttered the clearest statement of faith I have ever heard. "I don't know," she said. Her eyes were level, clear, strong. "But whatever is done with me will be *fair*."

Two years after our meeting, I came home to find a fat manila envelope in the mail box. I knew what was in it before I opened it. The return address read: Gerald Hollembeak.

I stood by the kitchen counter and opened the envelope. "Mom died May 20th," her son had written. "She spoke often of your summer together and the exchange of thoughts in the years after. She died with her children at her bedside and we shared laughter, tears, and politics. She was ninety-five."

The envelope contained letters I had sent to her, clippings of my columns, and photographs of my wife and children, whom she had never met. I touched the pinholes. The photos, apparently, had been attached to a wall or bulletin board. I put all of these things back in the envelope and thought about what I had learned from her—that all that really matters is family and friendship, and the best of life is written on pieces of torn paper.

The Strand
of Community

As a spider begins to build a new web, it comes to understand, by some mysterious sensing device, its new environment–how distant are the branches, how wet are the leaves, how stiff is the wind. As a parent, I am reminded each day of how different my sons' childhoods are from my own. The physical, social, and technological environment for children and parents continues to change at a rate that leaves parents and institutions grasping for some sense of stability. The branches have separated; some are gone entirely; electrical wires have replaced others; the wind is up. Strands of a new tensile strength are called for, but how strong? From what properties will they be made?

The Woman Across the Cul-de-Sac

MY WIFE AND I LIVED, FOR TWO SUMMERS, in a little town in New Mexico. We often visited a valley called Puerto de Luna, a place of economic poverty but spiritual wealth.

The valley's roads were made of dirt, and the Pecos River ran through it, but it often ran dry. The only dependable source of water was a little canal, a ditch really, which had been dug a hundred, perhaps two hundred years ago. Wars have been fought over such waterways. This one was tended by consent by the few families who lived in this valley, who raised chiles and children, generation after quiet generation.

The valley's efficiency was striking. There were not five tractors, there was one; there were not eighteen shovels, there were five or six. Our friends Nick and Isabel Raven never had to worry about rushing to the nearest city to buy a needed tool because it was likely that Juan or Jose Padilla next door had what they needed. When the Ravens left so Isabel could go to graduate school, Juan watched and tended their land, and their door was never locked. The essence of community in Puerto de Luna was the fine balance between independence and interdependence.

Today my wife and I live in another kind of neighborhood, a tract house in a suburban San Diego cul-de-sac. Finding a sense of community is harder here, less romantic, but still possible.

A friend of mine, a writer, theorizes that we write about what we are not good at. I suppose that is true sometimes. I often write about community and I am not good at it. For me, it takes conscious and reluctant effort to become involved in community activities. I am not a joiner. But it struck me the other day how interdependent my neighbor Kim and I have become.

Like me, she works at home much of the time. She creates gift baskets. Every morning one of us will call the other to offer to drive our grade schoolers, my Matthew and her Braden, to school. This is not a formalized car pool, so we are not really dependent on one another. We turn to each other when we need a favor, and the favor is returned.

I often have the feeling that Kim is driving more than I am, but she waves this off. "I'm not keeping score," she says. In a truly civil society, keeping score is not the point.

Kim, however, usually drives a bit more frequently than I do, particularly when I am traveling. December is Kim's crunch month. To prepare her baskets for the holiday season, she's working nearly round the clock, sleeping four hours a night. So, recently, I've tried to beat her to the phone. Kim protests, but who's keeping score?

Civility is contagious. I've noticed recently that Kim's daughter has begun saying, "Thank you, Richard," when I drop off her and Matthew. This does not seem necessary, but it is appreciated. Being her mother's daughter, she probably would say thank you anyway, but I like to think it has something to do with the sense of civility that her mother and I have cultivated between us. And

Matthew has begun saying thank you, too—at least to me.

I should add here that Kim and I are friends, but we really don't know a lot about each other. Perhaps a more descriptive phrase would be good neighbors, or, within the little universe of our cul-de-sac, good citizens.

It strikes me that such a relationship is not talked about much in our society. In a sense it has no name—the word neighbor, at least in the way it is currently used, seems somehow inadequate; the word citizen seems weighty and politicized. Perhaps we need a new word. Certainly, we do not teach our children about this role in school.

And yet, without it, there is no civil society—no web of connection to hold things together, to reduce stress and add intangible wealth. Without these connections, Puerto de Luna would have dried up and blown away long ago, and only the wind, and no memories, would have remained.

No government program alone can create these connections; no company can manufacture them, no money can buy them. But they hold us together, as people and as a people; these connections tend the communal ditches and get our kids to school on time.

Tara's Neighborhood

WHAT DOES THE WORD NEIGHBORHOOD MEAN TO YOU? The editors of *Cartouche Architectural & Design Review*, a publication of the Newschool of Architecture, a small architectural college with a predilection for contrarian thinking, asked the people of my city that good question. Essays were collected from architects, political leaders, and students at elementary schools.

The answers were revealing. One architect wrote: "Most often it is a set of automobile destinations which some groups hold in common. The wonderful neighborhoods we recall were pedestrian in nature, a visible link of public space. Only children and people without cars, know these places today."

In fact, some of the best answers did come from youngsters. One boy described neighborhood as a place with "a gas station so you won't have to go too far to get gas." Another grade school student defined a good neighborhood by what hers isn't: "My neighborhood is infested by gangs and drug dealers. My neighborhood has trash all over the streets and graffiti all over the walls. Every month there are about four fires in the building I live in. The cartoon neighborhoods on TV are a lot better."

Just when these answers were about to get me down, along came Tara, age ten. "A neighborhood is a group of houses that are next to each other," she wrote. "The people of a neighborhood work together or watch out for each other. They form groups to raise money for a playground or something like that. A neighborhood is not just a group of houses. It's a lot of people helping each other and giving things to each other."

Compare that to the answer sent to *Cartouche* by Brian Bilbray, then chairman of the County Board of Supervisors and now a member of congress: "A neighborhood is basically a sub-unit of a social-economic structure that is usually defined as a residential area, although it can be commercial too. It tends to be a sort of sphere of social activity where people identify it either to themselves or to other community members. It is basically a physical manifestation of the economic and social unit."

Brian, you should hire Tara.

Or maybe Tara should run for your office.

Our neighborhoods are being shaped not only by developers with no imagination or courage, but by our language. Too many Americans with the power to change things speak of community and neighborhood in a fatalistic, bureaucratic, throat-clearing way.

The future of community is also being shaped by our own muddled vision of what we want. Tom Evons, editor of *The Small Town Observer*, fled from big-city America to Bend, Oregon, several years ago, and has made a business, of sorts, advising people who want to escape to Norman Rockwell's small towns. But Evons has learned that small towns are just as likely as big ones to give way to strip malls and 500-channel cable TV. So now he counsels people to stay put if they can. "Think about what you want a little more deeply," he says. "A lot of Americans are looking for small towns, but what they need are traditional towns." By that, he means towns with neighborhoods that fit Tara's definition.

A few good people in neighborhoods from suburbia to the inner city are already planting the seeds for the growth of traditional towns inside big cities; they're sponsoring graffiti paint-outs, tree-plantings, block parties, cranking out neighborhood newsletters on their laser printers. But the more essential puzzle remains: What's a neighborhood? Jim Engelke, the Newschool dean, defined neighborhood as:

1. The place you grew up.
2. The place you remember that has something to do with your cultural heritage.
3. The sort of place that Garrison Keillor talks about on the radio every weekend.
4. The place that went away when you moved to California.
5. A place you would like to create but can't.
6. A state of mind.

Cartouche editor Doug St. Denis decided to answer the question himself in ("count 'em") twenty-five words: "It's where they call you by name at the cleaners and ask about the kids and don't ask for ID when you pay by check. E.T. said it better with one word, pointing his long finger toward heaven: 'Home.'"

Tara would probably like that answer.

━━━━

Aloneness and connection are like tides in the sea of your heart, separate tides, flowing in and out.

—M.C. Richards

Being a Good Parent–Neighbor

THE OTHER DAY I RECEIVED A CARD from some old friends who had just celebrated their fiftieth wedding anniversary. When I was growing up, Mr. and Mrs. Sebring were a kind of second set of parents to me.

They were the parents of my best friend, Pete. Decades later, I still can't bring myself to call them by their first names. They sent a photograph with the card. Both are in their seventies. Mrs. Sebring is beaming into the lens; the flash was a little too close, so her face is slightly washed out, but the outline of her smile is comfortingly familiar. Mr. Sebring sits behind her; his hair white and full, his face square and strong. His features seem to be a bit sharper now. He is smiling the smile of a man who has married well and lived to tell about it.

On the back of the photograph, Mrs. Sebring had written, "Waiting for God." It was a Sebring joke; it was her light way of suggesting that life is winding down and that, perhaps, something remarkable is about to happen.

Turning the photograph in my hand set me to thinking about what it means to be a good parent-neighbor, to be a dependable and available adult, to be there for neighorhood children without being intrusive. This is a skill I am learning. It is not, for me, easy. I am not very patient; noise bothers me. And I have had no training.

Or have I? As I looked at the photograph, I began to wonder what it was about the Sebrings that made them such natural parent-neighbors, what it was that I could learn from them now.

The first thing that comes to mind is food. Like all adolescents, I was hungry all the time but didn't always admit it. So Mrs. Sebring would often ask, "Hungry?" If I said no quickly, it meant no. If I hesitated, it meant that she should ask again. If I then answered, "kind of," she made a sandwich. I'm sure that the Sebrings and I communicated in code about other aspects of life, too.

Another rule that they lived was: Be there, but not too much. One of Pete's parents, and sometimes both, always seemed to be somewhere in the house. Mrs. Sebring seemed to live in the bright kitchen, half glasses hanging on a cord around her neck; Mr. Sebring was often in a little sun room with a portable television, watching sports, or he was out mowing and cursing the bald spots to which his grass transplants never took. The Sebrings didn't hover over us, but knowing they were around felt like a kind of silent light.

Also, they kept their troubles to themselves. That's an important guidepost for the good parent-neighbor. Laughter is always better than rumination. The Sebrings laughed at themselves, at their running jokes—at the coined words and awful puns that Mr. Sebring would bring to the table. The only thing I don't remember him laughing about were those bald spots on the lawn. They found pleasure in their children and in me, in getting to know my running jokes.

And they offered me the kindness of compliments. This was never overdone or gratuitous; I was not complimented for my neatness (that would have been a stretch) nor my conformity, such as it was, but for my uniqueness. When I was thirteen, I began to write a fishing column for the little community paper. They always read it. Mr. Sebring would repeat lines from it and laugh, and tell me that someday I'd write a book.

This was in sharp contrast to one neighborhood mother who, one day while driving a car pool, snapped her head around and told me, "You have a sick sense of humor." Or the other neighbor who decided I needed saving and carted me off to Sunday school but later disinvited me because I asked too many questions. Mr. and Mrs. Sebring liked questions more than they liked answers.

On the other hand, they knew not to ask too many questions—and to be appropriately grossed out when the occasion called for it. Children consider grossing out adults to be character building. It was pretty easy to get a rise out of Mrs. Sebring, when I would bring over a snake, or when Pete and I would haul heavy stringers of gasping, muddy carp back from the lake, or when we brought home bottles of leeches from the creek.

I'm sure there are other techniques for being a good parent-neighbor. For example, setting limits, or teaching children that they must be good children-neighbors. And, no matter what time a kid shows up at your door, never make a big deal out of it. Even if it's years later.

At the bottom of the letter, Mr. Sebring added this note: "As part of the family you should plan to stop over next time you come near Kansas City."

I reread that line several times.

Since I received their letter, I've been improving as a parent-neighbor. I'm trying to lengthen my fuse, trying to be there, but not too much, and so on. Yesterday I came home to find my older son and a neighborhood friend of his hovering over the stove. "Smells good," I said. "Making dinner?"

"Nope," they said. "Rat wine."

I was appropriately grossed out and tried not to ask too many questions.

Virtual Reality vs. Real Life

DO WE NEED PHYSICAL COMMUNITY ANYMORE? A popular idea in early science fiction was that humankind would one day evolve into a kind of floating consciousness—brains in space—leaving behind the messy, corrupt and annoyingly mortal human body. We're on our way, if you believe some of the devotees of the digital revolution.

Some of the newest communities—sometimes referred to as "virtual communities"—are electronic. On the Internet, America Online, and other computer networks and bulletin boards around the country, individuals mind-meld through a widening variety of online groups: electronic art colonies; SeniorNet, for older users; newsgroups for Scientologists and Macintosh- or foot-fetishists; twelve-step recovery groups (including at least one for computer addicts), and one online community called Shared Reality, in which the science fiction fans assume the identities of Cardassians, Klingons and other species.

At Hewlett Packard's Cupertino, California, office, employees started the Working Parents Network, part of the company's in-house electronic mail network. When Channah and Bill Horst's child died of SIDS (Sudden Infant Death Syndrome), they sought support and information about the syndrome—and the grieving process—from other online parents. Channah and Bill still marvel at the emotional support they received from the community of parents online. Says Channah, "What mattered was that we knew there were people out there who cared." One of the advantages of the electronic community, she adds, is that parents who communicate this way aren't time-bound; they can send and receive messages anytime they want.

But as helpful as virtual communities can sometimes be, they have their limitations. "When you begin using the computer to replace everyday experience; when you substitute virtual community for real community; when you take a virtual lover instead of a real one—all of this is a recipe for madness," writes Mark Slouka, a lecturer in English and popular culture. In his book, *War of the Worlds*, he describes the emerging battle between VR (virtual reality) and RL (real life). He does not mean to pick a fight with the crowds of people who communicate on the Net. His quarrel is with a relatively small but disproportionately influential group of so-called Net-religionists, including Bill Gates of Microsoft and Kevin Kelly of *Wired* magazine. "Some of them talk literally about creating an electronic heavenly city. They sound like St. Augustine."

Net-religionists tout the spiritualism of the hive, the increasingly interlinked computer systems that, as Kelly puts it, connect the "millions of buzzing, dim-witted personal computers" (that's us, says Slouka) into a one grand organism. And what will happen to the unhived? As one Net-religionist contends, they'll be "mere meat at the fringe."

How seriously should we be taking all of this? Slouka says very seriously. "When a significant number of powerful individuals—scientists, academics, authors, engineers, computer programmers—following the scent of a $3.5 trillion industry begin referring to the human body as meat (the expression is a common one among the digerati), it's time for those still foolishly attached to theirs to start paying attention." (Another on-line term for the digitally challenged is PONAs, People Of No Account.)

Of course, the digital revolution's dark side can be as over-hyped as its light side, but Slouka is right: There is something eerie about the lack of debate. "Like shined deer, we seem to be wandering *en masse* onto the digital highway, and the only concern heard in the land, by and large, is that some of us may be left behind."

Slouka (who, no fanatic, wrote his book on an old Apple II computer) admits that his apocalyptic tone may sound absurd. Most of us know the difference between the real and the virtual; we understand that a computer image of a two-by-four "does not a two-by-four make." But within a few years, such distinctions will be less clear. "We'll be able to pick up an electronically generated two-by-four. Feel its weight. Swing it around. Whack somebody with it. . . . We'll be able to immerse ourselves in an entirely synthetic world," he writes. In a thousand ways, from digital altering of photographs to on-line sex, we've already begun to accept fiction as the genuine article. He tells of a man who cheated on his wife for years in cyberspace, pretending to be a lesbian named Allison, of actual suicides which resulted when people were "bumped" out of their virtual communities.

We're withdrawing from RL partly because we're

scared. Parks and the streets and sex seem unsafe. But fear alone is an inadequate explanation. "It's not so much that we're afraid of what's out there as that there's no there out there anymore . . . . We live, many of us, in communities whose planners clearly had little or no interest in integrating the outside world into the lives of future residents."

I asked Slouka how he resists VR. Mainly through debate and small personal decisions, he said. And by walking. "My wife and I are habitual walkers. As a result, we probably know many people in our neighborhood, not all as friends. A couple weeks ago, I started talking with one guy—neighborhood kids love him—and he said Jews are the Devil's spawn. I pointed out to him that my wife, who was standing next to me, is Jewish. He about fell over backward to say that not all Jews are bad." RL is where real democracy happens. "My sense is that the constant rubbing of RL leads to a certain level of accountability and responsibility."

Such democracy is not possible on-line, where the forums are anonymous or provide for quick withdrawal. Slouka recommends a kind of new essentialism, a back-to-basics movement for daily life. Nothing radical here. Merely small, incremental gestures "as apparently insignificant as turning off the television now and then. Or going for a walk with a friend. Or spending the morning lying in a hammock. Or getting personally involved in some community issue. Or stressing face-to-face meetings over interoffice memoranda." The payoff? "Not utopia, certainly, nor paradise regained, but quite conceivably something like the sense of psychological well-being that one gets from coming clean after having become entangled in a net of lies and half-truths."

The best antidote to withdrawal into television and computers and whatever new electronic devices soon turn from useful tools into drugs, is face-to-face conversation; but this is easier said than done.

Many of us talk continually of finding community somewhere, of moving to it, of creating it. But the it is difficult to define. The it is a feeling that, once experienced, is always remembered. Here is what I remember. The stories, probably apocryphal, of Jesse James and Harry Truman, that informed my grandmother's neighborhood; the feel, later, of the sun on asphalt, the way it stuck to my feet as I ran up the street to a friend's house; the mythology of the woods, shared with neighborhood friends; the mother down the street who came to the door and stood in the shadows and said her son (who was big and aggressive) could not come out to play, and how she was killed in an automobile wreck and how, later, her son did come out to play, but his mind then lagged behind and he was gentle forever after; the stories, always the stories.

You cannot buy these stories at Wal-Mart; you cannot feel, on the Internet, the asphalt that connects you to your friends. Community is a finely woven fabric of sensory memories and stories; it is what holds us. My family, perhaps like yours, was a loving family, with troubles. But I always knew, intuitively, that no matter what was going on behind our doors, I could find some of what I needed when I walked outside. I could find the old couple down the street and adopt them as my surrogate grandparents, whether or not they wished to be adopted; and they would feed me cookies, and listen to me, and lend me the books that their grown children had left behind. There were, in our neighborhood, people who would report anything bad that I did on the street; they would pass this information on to my parents, not to the police. In school, I had mentoring, caring teachers. I had nature, to which I could go in solitude and find something larger. I was held by the mainly invisible strands of community. Now it is my turn to weave.

The Great Good Place

WHERE DO WE GO TO TALK? Where do we go to connect with people we know or don't know? Until coffee houses began to show up on every other urban street corner, few public places encouraged extended conversation. But now, the resistance lives! Its drug of choice: caffeine; its method of protest: conversation. If we're lucky and aware, the resistance could spread, in a variety of forms.

Ray Oldenburg, a sociologist at the University of West Florida, has written eloquently of *The Great Good Place* in a book by the same title. The phrase came from journalist Pete Hamill, who wrote that for a full life, aside from family and friends, "there must also be a Place—the Great Good Place that every man carries in his heart."

Oldenburg defines his great good places as cafes, coffee shops, community centers, beauty parlors, general stores, bars, hangouts. Great good places are where people learn to like one another for what they are rather than for what they own, where they meet by chance but also by design, where they sit a spell. Oldenburg calls these meeting points "the third place," the one between home and work. If we're lucky, such places help us get through the day. Or night. "Houses alone do not a community make," Oldenburg writes. Indeed, I am reminded that the soul of London resides in her pubs; Florence has its teeming piazzas; Germany has the bier garten; and Japan has teahouses. These are homes away from home; in cities that do not have such places, no one feels at home. That's the way it is with so many of us Americans.

Recently, I inventoried my great good places. I remember the benches in small-town Kansas where old men discussed the weather or women; and the cafes, thick with smoke and steam and politics and the crackling sounds of newspapers as they were folded back.

In the 1970s, the Sea Dawg Cafe on the Ocean Beach pier in San Diego was a place where fishermen and walkers and writers met and, over time, knew each other. As with many great good places, the key to the Sea Dawg was one powerfully social human being. His name was Craig Mueller. He is now a pilot; he was then a fry cook. He played the Beach Boys on the jukebox, flirted with the women, knew all of the regulars by their first names, drew out the shy or morose, and by force of personality made them talk.

One day during a storm he leaped with his surfboard from the pier and swam out to save a pigeon floundering in the high waves. Awestruck, the regulars stood at the window watching his bizarre heroism. He was a unifying influence, and when he moved on, the Sea Dawg lost its greatness.

Today, one of my great good places is a cafe called The Huddle. It's a place with old ceiling fans and gen-u-ine or at least good imitation Melmac dinnerware, and walls covered with photographs of stars from the 1950s; these are the photos of all the people who have never eaten at The Huddle. The waitresses there call you "dear" and tell you about their love and/or sex lives and point out people you should know and drag them over to you.

Across the street is a new great good place, the Better Worlde Galeria. (That "e" on the end of World is an irritant sure to lose the truck-driver trade, but no good place can be perfect.) The owners dreamed of a place where everyday people could share their talents. Judi offers gifts, pre-read books, coffee and a stage for singers and poets, artists and authors. Some nights, the neighborhood people pack in elbow-to-elbow. The owners have yet to make a profit, but they're getting close.

There's hope for great good places across the country. Coffeehouses are proliferating; some have electrical outlets for laptop computers. Could the urban centers in which we live, now so often empty of positive life, someday become "cities of conversation and cafes" as Ralph Waldo Emerson described Paris?

It's possible. Here's a three-quarters-serious idea: Offer a Great Good Place Tax Credit, and thereby reduce the need for so many psychologists and social programs. That would be a good investment in the glue that holds together what's left of our flesh-and-blood civilization, a way to support the resistance.

▆▆◣◥◣

One Wednesday night, five college students sat around a table at a coffeehouse near where I live. They gathered twice a week to do that most radical of things: They talked.

"When we get together, we don't talk about what's on the TV or what's in the papers, or the latest software," said Dennis, a literature major. "We talk about the last book we read." Dennis and Tony and Michelle and Jim gravitate toward the passionately political authors of Eastern Europe. The last book Dennis and his friends discussed was A Cup of Coffee With My Interrogator, by Czech author Ludvik Vaculik. The students are attracted to the movement that overturned the Big Lie of communism—not so much because the movement conquered a political system, but because it came from the streets, from the coffeehouses, from deeply felt and very private conversations.

"Today, the biggest problem in our society is fear," said Tony.

He's right. This isn't the kind of direct fear that people feel in a police state such as Iraq, but the subtle, generalized fear created by too much information and too little reflection. How many of us have enough time to talk? Serious conversation is a luxury, a packaged commodity: TV and radio talk shows with commercial breaks. "For my younger brother and his friends, there's still no place to go talk," said Michelle. "The houses are hot and small and the adults don't want a bunch of kids in the house, so the kids go sit on the curb at night and talk and then the police roll up and hassle them."

"There's a lot of power in just talking. But people aren't used to it," said Jim. "Dennis and I tried to start a writers' group and we had trouble getting people together. They're used to going to a party with music blaring so loud they can't hear. They're so accustomed to having every thought fed to them by TV that maybe they've forgotten how to talk."

"Partly it's economic," said Michelle. "Everybody is in such a hurry to get a career. The concept of hanging out and spending time—that's considered deviant. I learned about hanging out from my Italian friends." She grinned. "They say, 'Hey, we're Europeans—we hang out!' " But these young Americans are practicing the art of hanging out. "I go down to the Grove Cafe all the time and start conversations," said James. And he said he plans to take a couple years off from school, just to think about life before he goes hurtling into the non-conversant adult world.

"The most revolutionary thing you can do in this culture is to sit at a table and talk to people as if they're human beings," said Dennis. The others nodded. "Trash your TV and talk!"

The Bench

A FEW WEEKS AGO, MY WIFE DECIDED to redo the front yard. It is not a full yard, but a strip of nondescript succulents and a leaning eucalyptus. Usually when she decides to do yardwork, I hide, not entirely because I am avoiding real work, but because she is something of a threat with power tools. Forests have disappeared in her path. She likes to change things. I don't. I said: Why move to the manicured stucco wastelands (as you can see, I had resisted the move) if we were going to undo any of it?

I went inside and looked at my computer.

I came back out later to survey the carnage. She had ripped the succulents from the front of the little strip, and had planted a wood and metal bench next to the curb. It looked kind of odd out there. But my wife and I sat on it and looked out at the blank cul-de-sac. Pretty soon our kids started riding their bikes in circles in front of us. Then some of the neighbors approached cautiously and looked at the bench and at us. After we went back inside, we looked out the window. Two of our neighbors were sitting on the bench, and another couple was looking at them.

One reason my wife redid the strip of land and put that bench out there is that she is creative. She likes to take things apart and put them back together.

Another reason is that she was inspired by Suzanne Thompson, a woman I had written about a couple of years earlier. I had referred to Suzanne as a Suburban Guerrilla. One day, Suzanne looked around her rather sterile neighborhood and decided it was unsafe for kids; their parents seldom ventured out except to go to work. This meant that children playing out front were more vulnerable to unsavory passers-by. So Suzanne ripped up her front yard, built a courtyard with a river rock wall around it, put out some Adirondack chairs, and announced to her neighbors that they could use the courtyard as a place to socialize. She built it and they came.

When I visited Suzanne's neighborhood courtyard, the scene was like some Midwestern front-porch evening long gone, when cicadas would sing and fireflies would trace the murmuring discussion. Suzanne's neighbors sat with their drinks and the kids sat on the wall or played out on the darkening grass.

I admire good ideas, but my wife transforms theory into reality. She put the bench out there; the neighbors came. The block was already warm and neighborly, but the bench helped a little.

Another reason I think my wife decided to plant the bench was as a signal to the neighbors—but more to herself and her family—that we are sinking some roots. During seventeen years of marriage, we have lived in nine houses. Our moves were fueled by a variety of reasons: graduate school, work, our children's safety, schools, economics, escapism, and honest discontent with neighborhoods designed for cars, not kids. Yet the irony does not escape me: We left home to find home, and then wondered why we never felt at home. In this, we were emblematic of our generation and our parents' generation, too. During the 1950s and 1960s, when American mobility was at its peak, two of every ten people changed residences in a typical year. Mobility spiked again in the mid eighties, when 20.7 percent of the nation's population moved—when Americans scattered like swarms of bees. Much of this movement was in search of jobs in the Sun Belt, or because Americans believed they could find a better life in small towns. Some people found what they were looking for. Ralph and Muriel Keyes moved from San Diego to the picture-perfect town of Swarthmore, a suburb of Philadelphia. He says he was content in Swarthmore until the school district consolidated the neighborhood schools and a budget-cutting legislature closed the local high school.

"Our culture ripped the heart out of our communities when it decided that neighborhood schools were antiquated," he says. Next stop for the Keyes family was the small college town of Yellow Springs, Ohio. "We're fortunate today to live a few blocks from a locally controlled elementary school. We belong in this place."

My wife and I sometimes still dream of finding our true place. But the irony is catching up with us, as it is with so many members of our generation. We can't all move to small towns, even if they were as idyllic as we imagine them to be. Our restlessness is probably more hurtful than helpful to family and community. Maybe we should make more of where we are.

Now, according to the Census Bureau, a smaller percentage of Americans are moving out of their states than at any time since 1950. Why the slowdown? The economy is sluggish. The number of two-income households is rising, which means that families find it tougher to pull up stakes. And we're an aging population, so more of us find the idea of moving to be, well, tiring. We'd like to sit a spell.

So my wife and I sit on the bench. The neighbors sit on it. Passers-by sit on it. It is a place for conversation and a conversation piece, too, because public meeting places are rare in suburban tracts. The neighborhood kids use the bench as a kind of bus stop for their car pools. And sometimes they just sit out there. We see them clustered around the bench, their skateboards and bikes stilled for the moment. They sit and swing their legs and practice face-to-face conversation. Curtain pushed to one side, I watch them from the window and realize that we're not going anywhere soon.

A Survival Primer

LIKE MANY PEOPLE, I HAVE WATCHED with mixed emotions the outdoorsmen, as some police now call the hard-core homeless, push their chariots of debris up the hill near my house. I have felt pity, but I have also felt disgust and anger when they approach, hands out, with their reddened, bruised faces. I have felt fear walking my children past the park where they encamp, staring at us over their shoulders, eyes sunken in little caves. But I have also felt curiosity and wonder.

How do they live? Good God, to survive, they must be good at this—they must have tricks and talents.

So one day at a homeless drop-in center, I asked a group—a dozen men, a young woman with a four-month-old baby tucked beneath her coat, and the baby's young and toothless grandmother—about their survival techniques.

Storage is always a problem. If you save up some money, you pool it with your buddies and rent a ministorage unit. Shopping carts are the best portable storage units. If you're homeless, you find the shopping carts at recycling companies or stores. Some grocery store employees turn the other way as the carts disappear. "Our lives are in the shopping carts," says the grandmother's son-in-law, a kid wearing wrap-around sunglasses, a black fedora with *Corona Beer* written on it, and a blue wool poncho.

His wife says, "You keep everything in there, you know, little toys for your kids." If you have a baby or a small child and it rains, you put your child in the shopping cart and pull plastic sheeting over the cart. The problem with shopping carts is that when you go into a shelter, you have to leave the cart outside, and someone always takes it.

Your shoes and your blankets are your most valuable possessions, so you sleep with your shoes under your head. You put your money and pocket possessions in a plastic bag under your head, too.

"Someone can touch your body when you're sleeping and you don't feel it, but touch your head and you know it," says one man, wearing a black, studded leather jacket and an Army surplus canteen case (with a Walkman hidden in it), a very young and thin man the others call "Preacher." "He is the only pure one among us," someone says.

Always pull your sleeping bag or blanket over your head to protect yourself from the elements, particularly if you are a woman so that your gender is not evident. You sleep in dark-colored clothing. You carry your own toilet paper.

After a while, your body and mind begin to change: Your senses become finely tuned to anyone walking near you or watching you. After you sleep outside at night in the cold for a while, you need fewer blankets. These senses can dull if you stay in a shelter too long.

The buddy system is essential. "As long as we stay together, we're going to make it," says the young grandmother. You find places to rest and wash up. Libraries are known as safe places. A buddy watches your bags and shopping cart out front while you spend time inside.

You scout your territory. You find out right away where the gangs and the drug-dealing corners are, and you stay away from them, even if you're dealing drugs yourself. If you can make your way through the system, you apply for welfare or food stamps, worth a few hundred dollars a month, but seldom enough to rent a room.

Or you work for a living. You wait for someone to drive up in front of a shelter to hire you for day labor. "One guy came over from the Marriott Hotel, a subcontractor, and hired us to pull carpet. I was underage, but he hired me anyway," says Corona Fedora, "and I appreciated it."

Some of the men here have skills; one used to be a $16-an-hour union carpenter, "Local 906, Glendale, Arizona." You can hand out fliers or pick up day work with one of the private labor pools, which charge $9 or $10 an hour for your services, and keep over half. "Some of these labor services, once they take everything out, you end up with $1.40 an hour," says the carpenter.

You can storefront, as it's called, for one of the local private missions. You get into a van and you're driven to a supermarket or mini-mall, and dropped off with a bucket. This works differently from charity to charity, but the bottom line is this: You work all day for $10 or $15, plus a bed for the night.

You can also earn maybe $10 or $15 a day going through trash cans and picking up aluminum cans and bottles and cardboard and computer paper along the gutters. Some households put their recyclable trash out on the curb, knowing that the homeless will come by. You must be careful about going through trash cans. Sometimes you'll run into a syringe or a raccoon.

Cardboard goes for $30 a ton. One young man describes how he spent two days collecting a ton of cardboard, broke it down flat, filled four shopping carts that he had tied together, and rolled this contraption to a downtown recycling center. "Woman comes out, says she can't take it unless you bring it in a vehicle with a California license. So I had to leave the cardboard there. Later, I come back, and the recycling center, they'd taken the cardboard."

You can sell your blood, except that the market price has fallen. You steal. You sell dope. Not all homeless people, perhaps a minority, commit crimes to survive, but most of the ones in this group have done so at one time or another. "You sell crack to the Klingons," says the young grandmother. "Klingons, as in 'Beam me up, Scotty.' " She says one of her biggest customers in another city was a police detective. A $50 investment can earn $70. "I know it's wrong," she says. "But I have four kids and they're going to survive. If my son-in-law or daughter ever does it, them and me will go fist to fist. But the Good Lord says you gotta do what you gotta do. Don't get me wrong. I know I'm going to have to pay for what I've done, when Judgment Day comes."

These men and women talk of the kindness of strangers, of restaurants that hand food out the door, of strangers who hire them for an odd job, of good Samaritans who wish to remain anonymous.

I ask: How about all those "Will Work for Food" signs?

"Some are authentic, some of them just act homeless. They put on old clothes and collect money and buy drugs," says Preacher. "They're scammers. You never see these people in the food line. You can tell the scammers by their shoes: new $100 sneakers are a dead giveaway."

Ironically, you must appear homeless to be homeless. If you get too cleaned up, you get turned away from the shelters and, on the street at night, you'll get preyed on by the predators. Better to stay dirty. Or at least that's what these survivors feel.

It's a short trip to the bottom of the hill, but it's a long, long way back up, pushing those chariots of debris.

▙▚▚▚

The love of our neighbor in all its fullness simply means being able to say to him, "What are you going through?"

–Simone Weil

A Woman of Substance

WHERE DO YOU START? "From the beginning," said Sherry Buehler. She was sitting at a table in a back room at a local library. It was 9:15 on a Wednesday night. Only a few people were out there with the books. The place was filled with that soft hum that libraries share with cathedrals and courtrooms.

Sherry is thirty-six years old, a graduate of high school and a functional illiterate. Depending on whose figures you use, there are between twenty and sixty million functional illiterates in America—people unable to read or write well enough to get by in society, to read an adult book or the Bill of Rights or the poison warning on a can of Drano.

When Sherry asked for help from a county literacy program a year and three months ago, she could read at the second-grade level. On the evening that I met her, she sat next to her volunteer tutor and described what it is like to be functionally illiterate in America. When you begin to learn about illiteracy—about the frightening implications for the nation's economic and political health, and about the elaborate rituals people use to disguise their problem—then you can begin to understand the courage of people like Sherry Buehler, when they come out of the closet.

"I may be dumb, but I'm not stupid," she said, smiling slightly. "I knew I had to do something. I have a three-year-old boy, and I wanted to do it for him, but more, I wanted to do it for me." She is waiting for a certain day, and she keeps this day clearly in her mind. On that day she will be able to pick up a book, "not a children's book, but a book, and read it."

The journey toward that day began several years ago. She began the journey indirectly, not admitting to anyone that she couldn't read or write at an adult level, but taking basic aptitude tests at City College, using flash cards. "That was so hard," she said, because a couple of the people who administered the tests were "girls I went to high school with, or was with in Girl Scouts."

For a while, she received literacy tutoring as a part of a vocational government program, but then budget cuts wiped out the program. Then one night she was watching a TV program on which country singer Johnny Cash talked about his own early functional illiteracy—not being able to fill out job application forms—and she called one of the phone numbers on the screen.

And met Margaret Hamble.

"There are some things Sherry has learned to help her deal with life," said Hamble, her tutor, "words she needs to know for basic shopping, for instance. But she couldn't comprehend a simple newspaper article. I don't know what level Sherry was actually at when she graduated from high school, but a lot of times people who start out at a low level drop even further. In Sherry's case, she might have finished high school at the fourth-grade level and then regressed. If you don't use your literacy, you lose it."

Hamble, a retired kindergarten teacher and nursing

educator, is one of a small but growing army of volunteer literacy tutors. She volunteers through the county library's Project SURE (Strongly United For Reading).

She pulled out several manuals and opened them.

"See, we never repeat any lesson. One of the coping mechanisms of a functionally illiterate person is that they develop an acutely accurate memory; they can often repeat, by rote memory, what they have heard before. If we keep meeting regularly, Sherry may be able to read a mystery in another year."

The lights in the library began to go out. A few patrons straggled out, and Sherry and her tutor got up to leave. As they passed the counter, a librarian smiled and said gently, "Sherry, I got that book for you, the one you asked for. You let me know when you're ready for it."

I asked Sherry the name of the book.

"A Woman of Substance."

The tutor drove away, and Sherry stood outside in the dark and talked for a while. She said she wanted me to use her name, because it was important for her not to hide anymore.

"You fake a lot. Somebody hands you a letter and they say, 'Read this,' and you say, 'Well, I left my glasses at home.' You need to go the doctor's office, but it's so hard you stay away, because you can't fill out the forms they want you to fill out.

"You can tell when other people are illiterate and are hiding it. I can't really explain how, but you pick up little things. You know. And there's lots and lots of people out there just like me."

"In third grade, the school put me in a special education class. The teachers would come in and do their thing. I'd sit at the back of the class, real quiet, invisible, and they'd help the kids who knew more. They say you've got to have confidence in yourself, but how do you do that when you're cut down, cut down."

Did your parents know? I asked.

"Yes, but I don't blame them for anything." She stopped for a moment, and her eyes filled up with the light from passing cars. She suddenly began to cry. "I want to feel whole. Do you understand? I feel like everyone in the world is standing in a circle, holding hands, and I'm on the outside. All I want is to be inside the circle."

She finds it impossibly painful to read pre-school books to her son, because of the associations that she has with her own early years. The longest book she has read was *Angel Unaware* by Roy Rogers and Dale Evans; she picked through the bits and pieces of it that she could understand, and she cried when she finished. Someday she's going to be able to read *A Woman of Substance*, and, as she said, "Oh God, *Huckleberry Finn*."

Look, I said, so many people take books for granted or want to ban some them. What a special gift you'll have. Books will be magic.

"Yes," she said. "Magic."

Most of all she wants to read and write well enough to support herself and her son. She reached into her purse and took out a photo of her child, a clean-scrubbed little boy. In the photo, he was sitting in front of shelves filled with books, and an open book was on his lap. She had him pose like that.

It is, perhaps, too easy to blame public education, which has become the dumping ground for so many of society's problems. Many teachers are struggling to prevent the kind of thing that happened to Sherry Buehler. Still, institutions have a way of losing people—surely there are a lot of Sherry Buehlers growing up right now, invisible.

A few days after I talked with her, I called the high school that Sherry had graduated from. The teacher to whom my questions were referred did not want to be named.

Regarding Sherry Buehler, she said, "I don't have any idea what the graduation requirements were at that time. You're suggesting we can make a judgment about people who we don't know."

Would anyone there remember Sherry Buehler?

"We wouldn't be able to tell you."

Do some students still get through high school at a third- or fourth-grade level?

"No," said the teacher.

What reading and writing level, then, would be the minimum required to get through high school?

"I'm not going to respond to that because you're taking a totally hypothetical case."

But Margaret Hamble had responded to Sherry. They were two women of substance, weavers of the web.

‛‛‛‛

One reason community is so difficult to create is that we do not know if we want to create it. In 1973, Ralph Keyes began his book, We, the Lonely People: Searching for Community, with a dictionary definition of ambivalence: "Simultaneous attraction toward and repulsion from an object, person, or action." In a true community, we come in contact with people with whom we do not want to come in contact.

A few nights ago, I was walking with a friend in an urban neighborhood. Out of the darkness, a walking hanger of rags lurched toward us. I could not see his face. "I know you don't like me. That's alright, I don't like me either," he said as he approached. And as he passed he said, "You could be my friend if I knew what that meant." I think I know what he meant.

Community can lift us out of ourselves. It can also suppress us. Depends on the spirit of the community. Think of everything right about the isolated New England small town; think of everything wrong with it, too.

Skinwalkers

THE SKINWALKERS HAD BEEN BOTHERING MARY BEGAY. She stepped out of the mobile home into the morning glare. She wore a little white shell in her hair. Beneath her velveteen blouse, her body was still covered with paint. The medicine man had been here the night before and his blessing was still on her. He had made a sand painting in the ceremonial hogan next to the mobile home. He had laid Mary Begay (this is not her real name) down on the design and had painted her. He had built a fire next to her, and he and his assistants had sung in the smoke all night. This was done to make the skinwalkers go away.

The strands of our spirit are fragile and so easily warped.

"She is very tired," said her son, in his twenties. He spoke for his mother because she only speaks the Navajo language. He was sitting on a big piece of petrified wood in front of the mobile home. The Begay place is down a mud road far out in the pinon forest; this forest stretches across northern Arizona and New Mexico and a long way into the past. "We can't keep her away from her weaving. She won't eat right. She has lost a lot of weight." He said the skinwalkers were stealing her health.

Before I had gone out to Mary Begay's place, Jackson Clark had explained her situation to me. Clark, a respected and level-headed trader from Durango, Colorado, markets Begay's rugs. He told me that skinwalkers are a problem for some of his weavers, particularly the best ones. And Mary Begay is one of the best.

Night after night, he said, the shapes flit along the ridge in the moonlight. Covered with the skins of coyotes, the people build fires and howl and holler until they turn into things. They circle and circle and beat on the windows and the doors, and they cry: "Mary Begay, don't you weave no more, you're takin' money from the people."

Sometimes, the next morning, coyote tracks are found around the trailer. The Navajos follow the tracks for a few hundred feet, and the tracks, they say, turn into human tracks.

Clark once asked Begay's daughter, "What do you do when the skinwalkers come?" She had replied, "We blow out the lantern and huddle in the corner." Then Clark had asked, "Why don't you get a gun and shoot 'em?" And she had answered: "We can't do that! They might be friends of ours."

So, standing there in the morning light, with Mary Begay and her son, I looked at the ground. I cleared my throat. The ground was too hard for tracks.

"The sing cost us $300," said her son. The son stood up. He and his mother walked past two piles of fresh wool, draped over a pine pole fence. The wool seemed to glow in the light. They entered a tall shed next to the hogan, and I followed and stepped inside. It took a while for my eyes to adjust. Back where the light was weak you could see something incredible.

It went clear to the high ceiling, fifteen or twenty feet

up and just as wide. The design came into focus, bars of red and brown, patterns with the geometric intricacy of a silicon chip. The rug was a huge one, hanging unfinished on the loom. Mary Begay sat down in front of the rug, on an old Coca Cola crate, feet tucked under her skirt.

She smiled and the gold showed in her teeth. Her face was beautiful. She could not demonstrate the weaving for me, for she could not weave for four days, until the blessing ended, until she washed off the body paint. I asked what thoughts came into her mind as she wove.

"Only the weaving," she said, through her son. "I must concentrate."

The whole rug, all of its intricacy, springs entirely from her mind, said her son. No pattern is put on paper. She and her family clip and card the wool by hand and twist it into yarn on the ends of primitive spindles, a technology that pre-dates the spinning wheel. Sage is boiled to dye the yarn a mustard color; crushed walnuts are used for black. She comes out here at dawn and works through lunch until midafternoon, until the shed is too hot. Then she breaks until dinner time, and then returns to the shed and works until nine o'clock.

Sometimes at the loom she hears steps behind her and feels a skinwalker's hot breath on her neck, but when she turns around nothing is there. If the skinwalkers leave her alone, this big rug will take her a year and a half to complete. Near the end of the process, the warp of the rug will be so close and tight that her fingers will blister and bleed.

Does this rug have a special meaning for her?

Her son translated and she looked confused and said nothing. He said, "A long time ago the designs did symbolize things, now it's more of an abstraction." Then his mother said something soft to him.

"She says the rug has a meaning but she keeps it to herself."

Creating this rug must be more like creating a book than a painting. A painting is finished relatively quickly, but a book is a solitary work that goes on and on. I mentioned this and she smiled again and nodded.

In the past, she wove large rugs with her sister, but when the two of them worked together there were too many mistakes. So now she weaves alone. Three times she made errors on this rug that meant pulling out several feet of yarn and losing weeks of labor. This rug may be her last large one.

Is there such a thing as a perfect rug?

The question seemed to make her uneasy.

Her son answered: "The weaver places a spirit line in the rug, an imperfection through which all labor and concentration can escape."

If Mary Begay finishes this rug, it will sell for $25,000 to $30,000, and she will get $15,000 to $20,000 of that—which seems like a lot of money, until one realizes how much the world's top painters or writers would get for a comparable project. Still, among her relatives and neighbors—always at work on their own little rugs—her success creates intense jealousy.

So the skinwalkers come.

In recent months, Begay's vision has begun to fade. She must lean up close to the weave. She fears that the skinwalkers have come to take her sight.

In her culture, sharing is everything. To excel, to rise above your relatives and neighbors, is among the greatest of sins, and retribution must be paid for this. Yet Navajos (Dineh) are surrounded by the world's most competitive, capitalistic culture. And so they are trapped in this terrible contradiction; no wonder the Dineh die so cheaply from alcohol and suicide and other things.

"Navajo witchcraft thrives on envy," the trader had told me. "Hexes are placed on people here, and they die. They do die."

Driving down the mud road away from Mary Begay's place, I kept thinking about what he had said, and the strangeness of it.

Then it occurred to me that skinwalkers are not quite so foreign or so alien. They come in every culture; they just walk in different skins.

I'll bet you even know a few.

Protecting the Children of Others

THE AFRICAN PROVERB IS OVERUSED but true nonetheless: "It takes a whole village to raise a child." But practicing that principle forces us to ask some uncomfortable questions. For example, as parents, we get all kinds of advice about how to treat our children. But how should we treat other people's children? And other parents? Most of us have witnessed a mother or father physically or verbally abusing a child in, say, a supermarket. Are we witnessing abuse or discipline? Should we say anything to the parent? What about situations that fall short of abuse, but still constitute crummy treatment of a child? Should we speak up?

When my older son was eleven, he and I went to see *Jurassic Park*. We were sitting in the theater waiting for the movie to begin. The lights were up and the crowd was gathering.

Two young women and a man, who appeared to be in his late teens or early twenties, sauntered down the aisle. One of the women was holding a baby carrier with an infant about a year old. The young man was wearing a muscle shirt and a baseball cap, on backward. They walked to the front row and milled around as they figured out which chairs they were going to sit in. Eventually, the young man was handed the baby. I assumed he was the father. And I grew increasingly uncomfortable.

Depending on which expert is interviewed at the time,

the recommended ages for when a child should be allowed to see this film range between eight and eleven. After a while, I got up and walked down the aisle and spoke to the young man, who was still standing. "Excuse me, this is probably none of my business, but have you read the reviews of this movie?"

He looked at me.

I continued, "This child could be traumatized by this movie."

He looked at me some more with an expression that said, "Who is this guy? The Yuppie from Church? Mr. Self Righteous?" Then he said, "She's not going to watch it."

What? In the front row? Right under the screen? I looked at the baby. It was a little girl, dressed carefully in a lace dress. She was wide awake.

"But she'll hear it. And she'll feel it," I said.

He shrugged and turned his back and sat down. I walked back up the aisle to get some popcorn. When I came back, my son asked, "Did you tell the management?"

"No," I said.

He looked surprised.

"I already know what they'd say," I told him.

As the movie began and the wall of sound hit, I thought about the little girl, and about whether I had done too much or too little. Maybe my response was a class thing: I don't like muscle shirts. Maybe he's a good father. Maybe he and the mother can't afford babysitters (but could surely afford the movie tickets and the popcorn). Perhaps, if my own son had not been watching, I would have said nothing.

A few days after I saw the movie, I spoke with Kyle Pruett, a psychiatrist at the Yale Child Study Center, who said that an infant could probably handle the movie—toddlers were more likely to be traumatized. I found that hard to believe.

Infants are human sponges; they remember. As a five year old, I was convinced that a bogey man came from a shadow in my room every night, lifted me by the feet and shook me; I could only go to sleep after he did this. Decades later, when I was clumsily changing my first son's diapers, I realized where this impression might have come from: I held him by the feet and lifted his legs and bottom, wrestling the old diaper out from under him, and a new one under him. When I finished, he went to sleep. Surely the infant girl, surrounded by screams, under the jaws of the beasts on the screen, would remember.

Pruett did say that when he went to see *Jurassic Park*, a six- or seven-year-old girl in the row in front of him threw up; Pruett asked the theater's management if that was common, and was told that the ushers cleaned up vomit after almost every showing.

In the time since, I have thought often of the little girl, about personal responsibility, and about our culture's strange and contradictory assumption that nothing is private (just watch *Oprah*) except child rearing. Why are people more willing to speak up, in public places, to strangers who smoke, but not to those who mistreat or neglect their children? Perhaps more people feel justified in speaking up about smoke because they're going to breathe it; speaking up is in their immediate and direct self-interest. You can bet that had the infant cried non-stop during the movie, the audience would have felt a self-interest to speak up.

The difficulty is in defining self-interest. All of us are affected by how the children in our communities are raised. Yet too many of us treat other people's children similarly to how we treat the homeless. We walk around them. The current cultural belief is this: what parents do to their children is more of a private matter than what all of us do to the air.

While the community averts its gaze from other people's children, our legal system is moving toward holding parents increasingly responsible for their children's acts. In some communities, prosecutors now file criminal charges against parents who contribute to their children's delinquency by not trying to stop it, and some courts assign parents to mandatory parenting classes.

But what about the responsibility of neighbors who watch a child drift into gang activity and say nothing about it? Or adults who know that a child is buying drugs, and say nothing? Or movie theater owners who allow infants into such violent movies—does their behavior constitute a kind of child abuse?

Probably the theater owners rationalize their policies, while figuring their gross, by saying that the responsibility for policing these things belongs to the parents, and (the theater owners may think) if it's such a big deal, people in the audience would say something to the parents—wouldn't they?

It's possible that I was being overly intrusive or impolite when I spoke with the father in the theater, or that *Jurassic Park* was no big deal. But I wonder about that little girl, and about my hesitancy to err on the side of protectiveness.

Everywhere I go I hear people talking about rebuilding community. And their instincts are right. A sound family is tremendous advantage to a child, but it's not enough. The parent has to know that when a child walks out the door, there are others who care and will create a safe environment.

—John W. Gardner

No Fear

IN 1989, MOLLY WETZEL, A NO-NONSENSE businesswoman and single mother, became increasingly horrified as she watched her Berkeley neighborhood unravel and decay. She almost fell apart, too.

One day she found herself sitting at a table with her neighbors, discussing the best way to hire someone to blow up a neighborhood crack house, a center for violence and drugs.

Wetzel, a crisis management consultant for the University of California, had never considered herself a hothead, and certainly not a vigilante. But, like her neighbors, Wetzel had been pushed too far.

"At a bus stop, a crackhead pulled a gun on my fourteen-year-old son," Wetzel recalls. "My sixteen-year-old daughter was solicited by johns who thought she was one of the prostitutes who worked out of the crack house." Her son's grades began to slide. "He was frightened to death. He thought he had to carry a weapon to go to school. He told me the drug war had been won—by the dealers." Some of the older teens felt that they needed to join a gang to protect themselves. Every morning Wetzel would walk along her street and pick up empty syringes. "I was looking for a way out."

What she found was a way to weave the web.

For eighteen months, Wetzel and her neighbors appealed to police and the Berkeley city government, but to no avail. "That was when we started talking about burning the crack house down. We were going to pay a friend of a friend who was down from Oregon a hundred dollars to do it, and we were discussing how it could be done without hurting anybody." Fortunately, the group came to its senses.

One day, Wetzel read a newspaper article about a California appellate court decision that declared small claims court a proper place for settling disputes involving complex social issues. "A light bulb went on in my head. Eighteen of us from the neighborhood, ages three to sixty-five, sued the absentee property owner for destroying the peace and harmony of the neighborhood and preventing us from enjoying life and property. We wanted our lives back."

On August 29, 1989, Alameda County small claims judge Jennie Rhine announced that "no reported precedent could be found for a proceeding such as this, in which neighbors ... attempt to recover money damages in small claims court from the owners of the building for injuries caused by ostensibly criminal conduct of their tenants." Rhine said that "members of an aggrieved community may utilize the relatively speedy and economical procedures of small claims court to seek redress for a common problem." The case survived an appeal. Wetzel and the neighbors who had sued were each awarded $2,000. Within two weeks, the owner of the crack house evicted the drug dealers.

Today, the neighborhood is thriving—and so is Safe Streets Now!, a nonprofit organization Wetzel formed to help other neighborhoods fight crime by using small claims courts or the threat of lawsuits. Safe Streets Now! has twenty-three chapters in California, Florida, Louisiana, Massachusetts, and Washington. In California, the actions of Safe Streets Now! have resulted in the shutting down of 485 trouble spots, mostly drug houses, but also some liquor stores and motels that were hangouts for criminals. The key is for neighborhoods to come together as a team and file the lawsuit collectively. One person winning a small-claims suit can receive a maximum award of only $5,000. However, twenty people could collect $100,000. That leverage can force the property owner to stop the nuisance—before having to go to court.

Wetzel says that crime-infected communities with active Safe Streets Now! chapters experience a 15 percent to 25 percent recovery in real estate values. "In neighborhoods where people are afraid, they don't use the corner stores or the neighborhood markets, and they don't know each other. But after a successful Safe Streets Now! action, a nucleus of neighbors, a kind of village, forms. New leaders emerge. When they fight crime successfully, they realize that they can improve the parks and the schools—they can do anything."

In Oakland, teenagers involved in Safe Streets Now! went beyond direct crime-fighting: they created a Youth Information Center, which offered a youth employment hotline and a computer database of jobs. "The teenagers are learning how to raise funds, write grant proposals. As their power grows, so does their self-esteem," Wetzel says.

Other neighborhoods, in successful efforts to fight a recurrence of crime by building community, have sponsored tree-plantings and raised money to turn abandoned lots into parks. "After we got rid of the drug house in my community, I remember seeing all these kids running up and down the street," she says. "We had never known that there were so many children on our block."

Wetzel says the greatest lesson that children learn by watching their parents use the courts and other methods to fight crime "is that problems can be solved without resorting to violence." She's glad she rediscovered that truth, too.

The Culture of Renewal

NOT LONG AGO, A GROUP OF RIVERSIDE, CALIFORNIA, citizens, working with the county's school districts, concluded that the way to improve education wasn't to reform schools, but to reform the community.

This group included conservatives and liberals, educators, a building contractor, an insurance agent (and self-described survivor of the 1960s), a feminist activist in her seventies. On some issues, they had agreed to disagree—but they had found their common cause: the renewal of community. Today, with a mix of public and private money, they're busy creating family centers and neighborhood crime-prevention efforts and senior volunteer programs in the schools. Groups like this seem to have multiplied dramatically within the past four or five years. This growth doesn't seem to fit the current cosmology of despair or the current political/cultural spectrum; and the participants lack a hook on which they can confidently hang their hats. "I've felt ideologically and intellectually homeless for a long time," says the insurance salesman. What about Ross Perot's organization? "Close but no cigar," says an educator. "Too paranoid."

So where do they fit? William J. Bennett and Pat Buchanan talk of a cultural war in America; they say that the battle is between what they consider right-minded cultural conservatives and libertine liberals. They're right about the war; they're wrong about the combatants. The real cultural war is between the culture of narcissism and what might be called the culture of renewal, which is where these folks fit.

During the past two decades, the culture of narcissism assumed a variety of costumed identities; first came the benign, and often constructive, human potential movement. But the culture of narcissism moved on; it led to the abandonment of the traditional neighborhood and the rise of walled communities and private residential governments that offer elite services and private cops in exchange for personal freedom and privacy; it led to a political landscape that has less and less to do with our lives, and more and more with the vanities of handlers and pollsters.

The radical Religious Right and the intolerant Far Left are also part of the culture of narcissism; they cannot see past their own slim agendas; they pursue a kind of cultism, which is the group expression of narcissism. Even the self has been diminished; now we have narcissism's offspring, the culture of stuff—the deafening, electronic roar of commercialism without meaningful human content. The results? The starkest evidence is the emotional and physical health of children, who remain the canaries in this mine shaft.

But now comes some light: the growing number of Americans who have become increasingly dismayed by the disappearance of the public space, of community, of true safety. The culture of renewal shows up in some odd places.

During the '70s and '80s, the cafes, coffee shops,

community centers, general stores, the places between work and home where people can gather, put aside the concerns of work, and hang out simply for the pleasures of good company and lively conversations—these places virtually disappeared from the social landscape. But today, you can find them in a remarkable number of otherwise anti-social shopping malls, in the form of coffee houses; one is struck by the tentative sense of community in them.

Often unreported, or under reported, companies across the country are becoming more profitable by becoming more connected to community; many churches and synagogues are deciding to create support systems for parents and children, and experiencing a dramatic upsurge in membership; at campuses where, just a few years ago, social activism was moribund, half of the students—members of the so-called and much-maligned X-generation—are now doing volunteer work. From coast to coast, schools and neighborhoods and cities are tapping the capacity of ordinary citizens to reverse the slide toward crime and disintegration.

Today, over sixteen million citizens participate in some 20,000 crime-watch programs, and within the past two or three years, many of these programs have moved from merely reporting crime to preventing it by building community.

Renewal career tracks are emerging. For example, across the country, thousands of lawyers—most of them women—are rejecting the excesses of the adversarial justice system and becoming professional mediators, especially for domestic and neighborhood disputes. In effect, they are creating an alternative system of justice.

In many institutions, Americans are challenging the old directive style of leadership and adopting a more collaborative leadership. Foundations and community action groups, which only a year or two ago were turf conscious and duplicative, are beginning to pool their resources. In many cities and towns across the country, governments, foundations, and businesses are banding together to attack some of our most entrenched social problems.

"Two years ago, we weren't even talking about education as an issue of disappearing community," one Riverside educator told me recently. But during the past decade, we have learned something—that personal and institutional renewal comes in two forms: transitory or sustainable. Transitory renewal, focused on the self or on a narrow interest group, is neither lasting nor fulfilling. The cultural and political mistake of the '70s and '80s was the assumption that institutional or personal renewal could be accomplished without connection to community or to the next generation.

In contrast, sustainable renewal is wedded to community, to the public good and the public space. It exhibits a sense of generativity; it creates a web of support that helps other persons or institutions work toward renewal. This web will be for them when they falter, as each of us inevitably will. Across the country you can sense the emergence of the culture of renewal. It may not win, but it's growing, steady and sure.

The Strand
of Nature

The natural world is the larger sacred
community to which we all belong. We
bear the universe in our being even as
the universe bears us in its being.

–Thomas Berry,
The Dream of the Earth

Lion Hound

WE WERE STAYING IN A THREE-ROOM CABIN near the head-waters of California's Owens River. We could hear the quickening October wind moving down from the Sierra.

The boys were tucked into their beds, and I was holding *Lion Hound*, copyright 1955, by Jim Kjelgaard. The book was rebound in blue buckram canvas with a diamond design; the inside of the cover was hand stamped: Hocker Grove School Library. Inside the book was a makeshift bookmark, a torn-off corner of school notebook paper, yellowed with age. It is among the favorite novels of my childhood; I do not remember how it came to me, but I have my suspicions, and I have had it since junior high.

Now, on vacation, surrounded by knotty-pine paneling glowing in the lamplight, I read *Lion Hound* to my sons. "When Johnny Torrington awoke," I read, "the autumn dawn was still two hours away. For five luxurious minutes he stretched in his warm bed, the covers pulled up to his chin while he listened to the wind blowing through the bedroom's open window. Though the wind was no colder than it had been yesterday, it seemed to have a quality now that had been lacking then."

By today's standards, *Lion Hound* is ecologically incorrect. The central characters are a commercial hunter who collects the scalps and ears of lions for the bounty, and Johnny, the boy who wants to emulate him. The main protagonist is a killer mountain lion, which the two track.

As I read, I thought about a similar hunt last month in the Southern California mountains near where I live, how the ranger wept after she shot a mountain lion that had attacked a girl. The hills of California are still alive, as Kjelgaard wrote so long ago, with "tawny puffs of smoke" able "to break a bull's neck and yet are so secretive."

I glanced at the boys. The round glasses made my younger son's eyes seem even bigger. The older boy, then eleven, had tucked his face under the blanket, the better to see the Kjelgaard's mountain lion circling behind the boy and the hunter.

The next day, my younger son went into town with his mother and the older boy, who had told me he wanted to try to fly fish, walked with me to a stretch of the Owens to fish with barbless flies. As we fished, I thought about our relationship to nature, how different it can be from one generation to the next. Sometimes I wonder if mine is the last generation of Americans to share some intimate, familial attachment to the land.

Many of us who are now in our forties knew the edges of forest or farmland. Many of us had grandparents or other older relatives who farmed. Even a friend of mine, growing up in the concrete canyons of the Bronx, visited Uncle Max on his farm in upstate New York; my friend remembers the barn cat with the sandpaper tongue and a lazy day when he watched his father throw beetles into a spider's web.

My generation's adolescent fashions were work shirts, bib overalls, granny dresses, buckskin fringe; the cultural references for today's young people are almost entirely urban or video and seldom connected to nature or our agricultural past.

Recently, the Census Department released its annual report on the U.S. farm population and announced that, because the family farm is disappearing and only a small fraction of the population now lives on farms, this would be the last report of its kind.

But the strand of connection is not entirely lost. I may have had more intimacy with nature, but my sons have so much more contact with its larger dramas. As a boy I dreamed of bobcats, but never saw one; my sons live in a state where lions have returned in force. The clouds above Kansas were the mountains of my childhood imagination; my sons have already seen Mount Whitney.

As we fished, the eleven-year-old and I watched a great heron lift effortlessly; it seemed to remain stationary while the stream and the trees and my son and I seemed to sink. I watched my son lift the flyline in a long loop above his head, and I realized how rich his relationship with nature could become, if he lets it, and if I let him have it.

Under the cottonwoods, he had told me with firmness that he wished to tie his own leader. I understood, at that moment, that it was time for me to put some distance between us on the river. I moved downstream.

The evening came. After a while, he quit and walked with me as I continued to cast, and we saw the cruising shape of a big brown trout. When it was too dark to see into the water, we walked toward home in the cold, which was no colder than the night before but now seemed different.

We heard a noise in the bushes and looked up to see seven mule deer watching us, their heads and long ears silhouetted against the sky. We heard other sounds in the bushes where we could not see. We reached the gravel road, and an Oldsmobile drove up behind us and an old man rolled down his window and asked, "Do you need a ride or are you almost there?"

"We're almost there," I said.

We could see the light in our cabin. The younger boy and his mother were waiting. There was still time to read some more of *Lion Hound*.

Old-fashioned Reality

DO YOU EVER GET THE FEELING that nothing's real anymore unless it's on videotape? After all, who makes or raises anything with their own hands? Well, some folks still do, and they're at the county fair today.

The plastic tubing pulsed with white fluid pumping like blood through an aorta. The woman from La Jolla squealed: "Goat milk! I can't believe it! " She was ecstatic. "I've never seen anything milked!" What about cows? "No. Look at that! Fantastic!" She really was happy to see this county fair goat in its handmade wood stock, its udder hanging down full as a Nordstrom's shopping bag.

"Wonderful!" she said. Her name was Ruth Smallberg. "You only see this when you come to the fair." She was beaming. Another family edged up. The mother wheeled the baby stroller in front of the goat milking demonstration. The father kneeled down and snapped a photograph of wife and baby in front of the goat. Evidence. Real life here. It's come to this: handmade, hand-raised things now seem more strange and otherworldly than the yawning House of Mirrors, or the Crazy Dance spinning pods or even the Falling Star swing from hell.

"People ask a lot of really stupid questions," said no-nonsense Pam Ciesla, wearing a Desert Shield T-shirt. Muscled and tan, she was wrestling a goat. The goat was doing a backward rump toss through her arms. "People ask: 'Does it hurt the goat?' She locked the goat into the stock. "And they ask: 'How often do you milk 'em?' "

"How often do you milk that goat?" asked the man with the camera.

Ciesla hooked her thumb in his direction. "See?"

The question didn't seem so dumb.

Ciesla raises goats on a piece of property half in the country and half in the city. "My children don't have time to get into trouble. Too many chores. A year ago, we bought a membership to a video club, and we haven't rented a single tape. No time." She snapped the goat's teat into the tube. "I get half the football team at my house. They want to drive the tractor. I tell 'em, 'You want to drive the tractor, you load the manure spreader.'"

At the other end of the barn, Lois Schuck was spinning goat hair into yarn at a wooden spinning wheel. "Women are more inclined to ask questions, but men are more likely to linger. Maybe because it's mechanical." Schuck traded life in the fast lane for a goat farm in the country. "It blows my friends' minds. I used to wear designer clothes and work nine to five. Now I wear blue jeans and a hairpiece and work five to nine. No stress."

I took a break from reality. Out on the Midway, I bought a cinnamon roll and a carton of chocolate milk and sat down at a table and overheard a woman telling another woman her fantasy: that she would kill her husband if she could get away with it. I kept moving. The pavement seemed to jump with the base notes of rock 'n' roll; screams came from the Fun Zone. I stopped at the videogame parlor and met a twenty-three year old in a black baseball cap and black warm-up jacket. His moustache drooped down black and he smoked a cigarette with authority. He seemed very young.

He works at the fair, operates one of the rides. I asked him if he'd been over to the animal end of the fair. "Yeah, I like animals," he said distractedly. He was waiting to climb into Atari's new Race Driving capsule, a reality simulator. "See this one, you can pick the car you want, the track. It's like driving a real racer. You can feel the turn in the steering wheel."

He squeezed himself into the capsule, dropped two quarters onto a slot, turned the key, and was off. Watching, I felt my stomach roll as he dropped the roadster into third and flew over a hump and screeched into a turn—and the city was far off, glowing at dusk, and he leaned hard into a turn and the car heaved up, up, up and tipped the guard rail, and then he was flipping over and over, the windshield shattering.

Back in the agricultural section, I talked a while to a blacksmith and his wife, who work out of a rolling blacksmith shop. In Nickerson, Kansas, Ted Salyers is a working smith: a blade smith, a farrier, a coppersmith, a certified horseshoer. A few months a year, he tours the West's big fairs, hired to demonstrate the reality of smithing.

"Kids see in 3-D," Ted said. He was smudged and stolid and bearded. "They can see the thing take shape, but the parents can't." For years, he did iron work, high structure work, 280 feet in the air. Long after Ted became a blacksmith, he learned that his grandfather was a blacksmith. Sometimes when he works, Ted feels someone's hands guiding him. He met his wife a few years ago at the Bakersfield fair. She watched him pound and she came back to watch a few more times, and then she stayed. He took a red-hot horse nail and began to pound on it, the pounding ringing across the grounds, above the Midway's rock 'n' roll. "The fair's got too commercial, but people got burnt out on the glitz. Now they're coming full circle. People want to see the largest ear of corn."

Well, maybe. The agricultural and arts and crafts buildings aren't exactly packed now. Still, while the numbers might not be there, the intensity is. He handed the nail to his wife. "Hot?" She shook her head. She checks his work for him because his hands can't much feel heat or sharpness anymore. He handed it to me. He gives these away. It was a key-chain ornament, with the delicate face of a wizard.

"We're right next to the calf-birthing pen," he pointed out. Nearby, a calf was standing, wobbly, its cord still hanging wet and red.

"One o'clock yesterday, the fair PA system announced a calf was being born. Sixty-thousand people. Seemed like most of them stampeded this way. They come buckin' outta the barn. To see a calf being born! Can you believe that?"

Nature comes in many forms: a new calf steaming, a pet that lives and dies, a woods with beaten paths and stinging thistles. Whatever form nature takes, it offers children a world separate from parents and older than them—a kind of greater father and mother; it gives children a sense of their place in time. Unlike television, nature does not steal time from adults or children; it augments that time, makes the time fuller, richer. And for those children for whom family life is destructive, nature can offer healing.

Nature also serves as a blank slate upon which children may draw the fantasies supplied by the culture; nature nurtures creativity in children, in part by demanding visualization, the full use of the senses.

We do not fully understand how much we wound children by our destruction of nature. The preservation of nature should be among our essential goals when we weave the web of life, not only for the protection of the least tern, but also for the mental health and the creativity of the next generation. And this stewardship should be focused, not only on mountains and deserts, but on the woods and fields at the end of the block.

All Our Relatives

SOMEDAY ROBERT STEBBINS MAY BE KNOWN as the man most responsible for saving what was left of the California desert. He is an old man now, and already something of a legend. Before I went to see Stebbins, I did some background research.

I walked over to the mall to pick up a copy of Stebbins' book, *A Field Guide to Western Reptiles and Amphibians*, which he wrote and illustrated. For twenty years, his book has remained the undisputed bible of herpetology, inspiring countless youngsters to chase snakes as a career. At the Nature Company, a young, bearded salesman told me Stebbins' *Field Guide* was sold out. He asked if he could order it for me. "No," I said, "I'm interviewing Stebbins next week."

"You're interviewing Robert Stebbins?" he said. We were surrounded by Eternally Cute Sea Otter T-shirts and Inflatable California King Snakes. The way he said it, you would have thought I was going to interview Madonna. Or, better yet, the Beastie Boys. "He's the greatest," said the young man, who, as it turned out, was a recent college graduate in herpetology. He had once attended a lecture by Stebbins. "Other people paint animals," he said. "Stebbins captures their essence."

A week later, I was walking with Stebbins through the bowels of the Museum of Vertebrate Zoology at the University of California, Berkeley. Retired, Stebbins remains a professor emeritus and curator emeritus of the museum.

"We've got to teach people that we're related to every living thing, even the AIDS virus. Maybe that's an unfortunate example," he was saying. Bald, agile, he has a young man's gait. "We're not sure viruses are alive." He was winding his way, in the dim light, through rows of oak chests. Off to one side was a great, wooden door to a vault, with a handwritten warning: "Bone Room—Do Not Lock Door Until Certain No One is Inside."

This museum is primarily a research museum, and we were in a section seldom seen by the public. From the chests, he pulled narrow drawers to reveal neat rows of long-dead animals; some of these specimens, now extinct, were captured in the nineteenth century. Their innards were scooped out, their skin dried and body cavities stuffed, and their skulls placed next to them in small cardboard boxes. He held a quetzal parrot gently in his hand. It had lain fifty years in this crypt, but now the bird's feathers caught the light from a distant window and the colors flew.

He put the bird back, closed the drawer, walked into his dusty office, and sat down at his roll-top desk. On top of the desk was a statuette of a monkey contemplating a human skull. Stebbins told this story:

"In the late 1960s, I began taking students out to the desert to snare lizards and call in the owls. One morning before dawn I was lying there listening to a horned lark, feeling at peace with the world. Then I heard this roar approaching as the sun was rising. Motorcycles tore up, racing around and around us, sticking an American flag in the ground as a rendezvous. We looked at the damage after they had gone. I felt as if I had lost my mother."

During the next ten years, Stebbins and his students would drive to the desert areas frequented by all-terrain vehicles (ATVs) to document the destruction they cause. In the evening, they would use big push-brooms to create long swaths, and in the morning, they would record animal tracks. Over the years, 90 percent of invertebrate animal life—insects, spiders and other arthropods—were eliminated. "By now, most of the vertebrate life has probably disappeared in the often-used areas, even as the sport spreads."

The most recent threat is to isolated mountain areas and dunes that until recently have remained relatively undisturbed. These areas "rival the Galapagos Islands for their ability to unravel the secrets of evolution."

He dropped scores of slides into an old viewer.

"Look," he said. "Ten years of before-and-after photos."

Grooves and scars, tracks that will remain for centuries. Desert crust ripped up by rubber tread, and great clouds of dirt rising high into the atmosphere. Bomb bursts of fine sand dunes. A desert tortoise, shot with a gun, with a single tire track cracking its back. Aerial photographs taken near Blythe, California of ancient and mysterious Indian intaglios, carved images so large that they can only be perceived from the air. Across the flanks and back and head of a deer-like intaglio: claw-marks left by ATVs.

For eight years, Stebbins labored as liaison between

scientists and the Bureau of Land Management, "trying to get them to turn the screws on off-road vehicles. But they haven't done enough." Of course, the ATV lobby, powerful in California, has its arguments, but the continued encroachment on desert lands, even after they have been restricted, is beyond rationality. Stebbins says it amounts to a kind of species self-hatred: lemmings bashing themselves against a wall and calling it fun; the environmental equivalent of slam dancing. In Missouri, the latest fad is river riding: gunning big-wheeled all-terrain trucks down the middle of rural streams. "If only these people knew what they were doing."

Suddenly Stebbins' mood brightened. He told of a recent trip to the desert, where he taught a powerful U.S. Senator how to call in owls. I asked Stebbins about this peculiar talent, which he taught himself as a boy. He cleared his throat, contorted his mouth into a sucked-in "o" and somehow made his chin disappear.

Ho-ho-ho-ho-ho-ho-ho.

He grinned. "Great horned owl." At one time, Stebbins could attract thirty species, including a Colombian crocodile, which he called at night with a little sneezing sound. "Up to my chest in water, had a headlamp on. I could see it coming, eyes glowing red." The animals come to him, he said, not out of affection, but to protect their territory. (I was struck by the thought of the Senator taking his new skill to the Senate floor.)

So here is the reason Stebbins instills such awe in his students: Part of him is still a boy ranging through the Santa Monica mountains, calling in the owls. For him, the world is still magical, even if for some boys and some girls the magic has been buried beneath the tire tracks.

"One time, I was out looking at the ATVs. I saw these two boys trudging up a dune. I went running after them. I wanted to ask them why they weren't riding machines—maybe they were looking for something else out there.

"They said their bikes were broken. I asked them if they knew what was out there in the desert, if they'd seen any lizards. 'Yeah,' one of them said, 'But lizards just run away.' These kids were bored, uninterested.

"If only they knew."

The $70 Lizard

LET ME TELL YOU THE STORY of the $70 lizard. Not long ago, my family and I drove up to the Laguna mountains, east of San Diego, for a weekend outing. On the way back, we stopped at a desert outlook.

Jason, ten at the time, and I climbed down the rocky embankment to an outcropping and dangled our legs over the edge. We watched a raven peck its way up a gully.

Sitting there, I thought of my father, using a fishing net to chase collared lizards across rocks next to Bull Shoals Lake in Arkansas. These big-headed collared lizards, which ran upright, looked like little Tyrannosaurs, and, pound for pound, were almost as vicious. We took one home in the '53 Dodge, put it in a terrarium, and I watched it for hours, imagining prehistoric carnage.

I remembered how, in the Midwestern spring, box turtles would crowd the country roads in some kind of sexually stimulated migration, and puritanical cars would flatten them. Now and then on the road you'd see a spinner, a box turtle on its back, clipped by a car ahead, spinning so fast that it was a blur. My father would slam on the brakes and my mother would jump out and save the spinner. The car floor beneath my feet would fill up with box turtles. We would take them home and keep them for the summer in a chicken-wired hole in the back yard, a turtle pit my father had dug for me, and now, I understand, for him.

My father is gone now. Jason and I sat on the edge and watched fat, spiny black lizards dart across the rocks far below. After a while, my son and I climbed back up the embankment in the heat, where my wife and Matthew, who was four then, were waiting.

"We've got a surprise to show you," said Kathy, smiling. Matthew was jumping up and down. From the shade beneath the car, she brought out a can. She reached in. On her palm rested a two-inch-long baby horned toad, or, as it is formally known, horned-toad lizard. Like collared lizards, horned toads look prehistoric. They have fat bellies, large heads, and quizzical eyes. Unlike collared lizards, they're gentle. I thought of my father. As a boy growing up in New York, he once sent for a mail-order horned toad. When it finally arrived, he took it out of the box. It sat in his hand immobile. Maybe it needed fresh air. He took it outside. He put it on the front stoop. He watched it for about an hour. Maybe it was dead. He poked at it. It took off in a flash, maybe back to Arizona.

Remembering my father and his lizard, I said to Matthew and Kathy, "Great! We'll take it home."

She sighed. "I don't think so."

"What?"

"Matthew and I have already talked about it. The right thing to do is to look at it and then let it go."

I protested. I lowered my voice and acted macho. I pleaded. I whined. Nothing worked. Then Matthew started crying. I rested my case.

"Rich, I thought you were an environmentalist," she said.

Well, that got me, right below the ideological belt. She and the boys took the lizard over to a bush. "I wish we could keep him, too," she said, putting the lizard on the ground. It sat there for a long time. Matthew poked it. It skittered off into the base of the bush.

We were silent all the way home.

After unlocking the door, I went in and grabbed the Yellow Pages and called Pet Kingdom. "Do you sell horned-toad lizards?" I asked.

"No, they're a protected species. It's illegal."

I looked at my wife. "Do you sell anything like horned-toad lizards?" They did.

So the boys and I headed for the pet store, which was offering specials on collared lizards and crevice spiny lizards. The crevice spinys looked vaguely like horned-toad lizards, though much bigger. They were $29 "with the purchase of an appropriate tank, heater, and so on."

By the time we added up the etc., we owned a $70 lizard. We took it home. I was feeling much better. "You did the right thing, Kathy," I said to her, expansively.

She smiled, and graciously said nothing about the cost. We set up the terrarium and fed the lizard some crickets, also bought at the pet store. Matthew was impressed but soon wandered off to the Nintendo game. I watched the lizard for a long time, imagining prehistoric carnage.

A few weeks later, the lizard wasn't moving. We took it out back. Matthew poked it. Nothing happened. We buried it wrapped in tissue.

"I hope you're not too sad," I said to Matthew. He

patted my arm.

"Can we go get another lizard?" he asked.

"Not right away."

He brightened. "Then can I have a *mouse?*"

◢◣◢◣

As I look back on fully seventy years of awareness and recall the moments of greatest happiness, they were, for the most part, moments when I lost myself all but completely in some instant of perfect harmony. In childhood and boyhood this ecstasy overtook me when I was happy out of doors. . . . A silver haze shimmered and trembled over the lime trees. The air was laden with their fragrance. The temperature was like a caress. I remember–I need not recall–that I climbed up a stump and felt suddenly immersed in Itness. I did not call it by that name. I had no need for words. It and I were one. Surely most children are like that. I have retained that faculty through the years. As a result of this sense of continuity of personal experience, the early pattern of thought is established, and subsequently it becomes a method or technique.

–Bernard Berenson, in his autobiography

Connecting Children to Nature

AS A BOY, I HAD NO AWARENESS that my woods were ecologically connected with any other forests; nobody talked
about acid rain or holes in the ozone or global warming.
But I knew my woods and my fields, knew every bend in
the creek and dip in the beaten dirt paths. I pulled out
survey sticks in advance of the slow-motion bulldozers
that moved, ever closer, like an armored division. I wandered these woods even in my dreams.

But in the last years of the twentieth century, for many
kids, maybe most, this relationship has reversed. Today,
children express extraordinary awareness of the global
threats to the environment, but at the same time their
physical contact, their intimacy with nature, is fading. A
while back, a fourth-grader told me that he likes to play
indoors better, "cause that's where all the electrical outlets are."

As a journalist, I hear from adults painfully aware of
this transformation. "I sometimes feel like the last of a
dying breed of young people who grew up right as the
technological boom was really beginning to bust out all
over, in the early '70s," wrote Janet Aldrich, who works
with inner-city kids in Washington, D.C.

"I weep for the vanished nature lost to children today. I grew up in the '50s wandering daily through the
wonderful woods near my house," wrote Val Ernst of
Seattle. "Even today I feel safer and more at peace out in

the forest than inside a building. I now direct two school-age child care programs. I am fiercely determined to provide copious opportunities for these kids to have regular personal interaction with trees, streams, meadows, etc."

In 1978, Thomas Tanner, professor of environmental studies at Iowa State University, conducted a study of environmentalists' formative influences—what it was in their lives that had steered them to environmental activism. He polled staff members and chapter officers of the National Audubon Society, the National Wildlife Federation, the Nature Conservancy, and the Sierra Club.

"Far and away the most frequently cited influence was childhood experience of natural, rural, or other relatively pristine habitats," according to Tanner. For most of these people, the natural habitats were accessible nearly every day when they were kids, for unstructured play and discovery. "Several studies since mine have supported my findings," he says. "But for some reason, you don't hear many environmentalists expressing much concern about the intimacy factor between kids and nature."

Still, an increasing number of parents—and a few good schools—are realizing the importance and the magic of providing hands-on, intimate contact between children and nature. Something's about to hatch. Many of us are already acutely aware of our own disconnection to nature, amplified in our children, and the need to reweave that connection. Much of this reconnection happens on the personal and private level. But institutions can help, too. Around the country, schools and museums are stepping up their efforts to connect children with nature.

At a school near where I live, three kids and four adults moved down the canyon path to where city sounds were submerged in cool silence. "We get the classes down here touching, tasting, smelling, tracking. It's hard to get twenty-six kids to be quiet, but we do it," said Dennis Doyle, who at that time was principal of Torrey Pines Elementary School. "They're ripe for it." Doyle believes that encouraging students to experience more intimacy with nature, more hands-on experience, will be a better way to introduce children to science than reliance on textbooks. In fact, during the nineteenth century, nature study, as it was called, dominated elementary school science teaching. While nature study was shoved aside by the technological advances of the twentieth century, an increasing number of educators believe that technically oriented, textbook-based science education is failing. At Torrey Pines Elementary, sixth-graders were scoring poorly on the hands-on science test given nationwide by the National Teachers Association. So Doyle and his staff decided to make a radical shift.

They decided to restore the canyon behind the school to its natural state, and to create an outdoor classroom and nature trail. The idea was twofold: to help kids experience the kind of intimacy with nature that many of their parents enjoyed, and to improve science education—to make it immediate and personal.

On their forays into the canyon, work teams of kids, teachers and parents ripped out the plants not native to this area, including pampas grass and Hottentot fig (incorrectly known as ice plant). On our walk through the canyon, Diana Snodgrass, a docent at Torrey Pines State Park, explained that Hottentot fig probably was brought to the area on ships, by Spanish sailors, as an edible and hardy plant rich in vitamin C, useful in the prevention of scurvy. Many people believe the big-fingered Hottentot fig prevents soil erosion, but because of its weighty water content, the plant also can pull down a steep embankment. So in this canyon, for this fig, the jig's up.

"When some of the Hispanic parents come down here, they immediately recognize certain herbs and medicinal plants, including one that's added to beans to stop flatulence," Snodgrass added. She said this herb was also brought here by the Spanish, a practical people, on their close-quartered ships.

The school project will return this habitat to native plants, such as Torrey Pines, yucca, cacti and chaparral. The school children are now growing seedlings in their classes for later replanting.

"The skeleton is down here," said Doyle. He pointed to a mat of dried hair and mummified meat.

"Perhaps," said volunteer Heather Wood Ion, who wrote the grant proposal, "we should frame that opossum and hang it on the wall in Dennis' office." Doyle grinned and the kids giggled. Then Ion leaned over the corpse. "Can you see the backbones?" she asked. "They hold the spinal cord, which is attached by ligaments to the skull. Like this." She touched the base of her own skull, and the kids immediately touched their own. Surely this lesson will last longer than any anatomy lesson learned from a textbook.

Another benefit of the project is parental involvement. "Last weekend, we had about thirty people working in the canyon," said Doyle. Half of the parents were from wealthy nearby neighborhoods; the other half were from the less affluent neighborhoods from which some of the students were bused. They were hacking away at the pampas grass, using machetes, all pushing and pulling together. That kind of experience binds people together more than any formal integration program."

For the three kids, Susan, Darren, and Sean, this was their first hike deep into the canyon. "It's fresh!" said Darren. The others nodded. "I used to go down to a canyon, about a mile long, near my house," added Sean. "I found this little cave; I'd sit in it and wait for something to come by. But I got a sore on my leg from some glass, so my parents don't want me to go down there now."

There's a contradiction here. How can any child's experience of nature be truly natural if an adult is hovering nearby? Doyle acknowledged this contradiction. But he tried to keep the experience as natural as possible. For example, he asked the kids questions—but he didn't answer the questions.

"Look at these twigs," said Darren. "It looks like one twig is dead, but one is alive."

"Why do you say that?" asked Doyle.

Sean launched into an elaborate and erroneous theory.

"That's an interesting theory."

Darren trailed after Doyle, excitedly checking other twigs. In this special classroom, imagination is more important than technical precision.

Now, standing on a ridge overlooking the canyon, I asked the kids: If you had five hours to do anything you wanted down here, no adults, just your own free time, what would you do?

"I'd like to hike all the way down the side," said Sean. "So many places to go. Five hours couldn't cover it." Darren thought for a moment, then said, "I'd use that time to take out more ice plant, to do whatever I could to keep it the way it should be. Like forever."

Nature ignites the genius of everyday life. "I would define genius as an evolutionary phenomenon, at the biocultural levels, beginning with the natural genius of childhood and the 'spirit of place,'" writes art historian Bernard Berenson. This makes sense; I suspect that most gifted people had some kind of transcendent experience in nature during childhood, and that this experience amplified their senses throughout their lives.

The spirit of place informs all our connections and relationships: family, friendship, and community. The spirit of place is not necessarily attached to, or entirely dependent on, the actual molecules encountered. The spirit of place is an enlargement of the real. How many of us, growing up in the flat Midwest, spent long hours on our backs listening to the wind rush from some distant sea through the grass and through us as well, and we heard in that air more than air; we heard God's chorus. We did not need mountains then, we had the clouds. A place was more than a place, when we were young; a place was a spirit. And still is.

Flyover Land

DRIVING SOUTH ON INTERSTATE 135, from Salina toward Arkansas City, I can see the giant rolls of hay that look like mammoth shredded wheat, and the long hedgerows of Osage orange trees planted as windbreaks during the Depression, now taller than I remember them.

Cream-white waves of tall grass. The wind coming across, always the wind.

This is the flyover land. Jets stream far above and people with briefcases and laptop computers look down and feel glad that they are not driving across this seeming emptiness. But when you drive across north and central Kansas, particularly if you are originally from this country, you do not feel the fatigue and the tension that accumulate on urban freeways.

The land is soothing and nurturing and layered with mystery.

Riding a bus across the state in the 1960s, I remember awakening suddenly, a bit disoriented, sitting up in the night to see long lines of flame stretching across the Flint Hills prairie, annually burned by ranchers. The lines of flame were galactic in their brilliance and desolation and beauty. Now, more than two decades later, the miles fly by.

Kansas seems fresh and clean compared to much of the rest of the country: patches of dry grass, and deep green ravines filled with trees, and combines on the horizon with the black earth swirling up into the atmosphere.

Now and then a half-hearted dust devil skips across the fields, and nodding pump jacks suck oil from beneath the land, their heads and necks moving up and down like prehistoric birds.

And of course, the clouds, always the clouds, high cumulus clouds spaced almost evenly across the sky, snow white on top and slate gray underneath. Past Lindborg and Gypsum toward Assaria, the sky a mirror of the land. Black birds clustered on the tops of sorghum.

So much of this land was lifted up during the Dust Bowl years and flung into the air and so many of the people landed in California.

Now the fields are ripe, rich in color—the rust of sorghum, the gold of cut wheat, the deep black of plowed earth and all the lines of trees in different shades of green; some turned by sudden shadows from moving clouds tar black against yellow grass, cedars and hedgerows leaning like herds of something forgotten into a wind that has stopped.

Stuckey's, Texaco, long lines of rail cars stopped on the prairie. More trees here than a century ago. Now past the Smokey River where the land flattens out even more.

Few places in Kansas are truly flat. Only in the most western regions does the line cease to move in curves and jumps and serrated ridges. Only there does the line of the horizon like the green line on a heart monitor grow steady and flat. In most places of Kansas, the land is like some long symphony with repeating themes and with subtle notes but never monotony.

Away from the cities, square-box white farmhouses stand up large with lonely dignity, and of course the windmills and the silos are there and the white lines of dust moving upward from the horizon.

At night this land turns endless and bottomless. On some nights there is nothing but stars. On other nights frighteningly violent storms and hours of calm just as frightening, and then sometimes God's fingers or perhaps the devil's claws reach down and, twisting, scrape across this long, sinuous back with a roar that one can only describe if one has heard it.

And the smaller moving mysteries. On the road ahead, and then for 200 miles, small yellow caterpillars inch across the road.

Painted box turtles move en masse too, especially in the spring. In one Kansas town a few years ago, the citizens were split between those who wanted to make the box turtle the state animal and those who didn't, and the turtle opposition, called "poppers," would drive out on the highway at migration time and intentionally drive over the turtles.

This land heaves itself up. Migrations of insects, reptiles, people seem to move up from this land and outward.

I remembered: One night in 1969, driving home from a girlfriend's house outside of Hutchinson, the wheels of my car began to slide on the road.

There were no clouds in the sky; it was filled with

stars. But I nearly lost control of the car in the slide. In my headlights I could see blips and blurs like a rain of hail or a swarm of locusts—it was neither. It was frogs, a hatching of frogs, or toads, I do not know which. But thousands of them were hopping, flying across the road and my car was sliding on them.

The flyover land is breathing land.

This is where East becomes West. This is where the sensuous hills of Kentucky and Illinois and Missouri meet the hard, spare rockiness and dryness of the masculine West. These are the plains of fertility. This is not the heartland, really. This is the seedland. Food Phone Gas, next right.

Everyone Has One True Place

MOST PEOPLE WOULD LIKE TO FIND their one true place, their ecological niche, their island of belonging. Now and then you meet some lucky person, like Barbara Remington, the herb lady of Oregon, who has found such a spot. This does not mean she has no complaints. One afternoon, the herb lady was complaining about slugs.

"The helicopters fly over and drop 'em," she says, grinning a mock-conspiratorial grin. "Which isn't far from the truth." Birds eat slug eggs, and when birds scatter their droppings, they also deliver little slug-egg warheads. But raining slug eggs is part of the nature of things at the Dutch Mill Herb Farm near Forest Grove, and the nature is good.

Her ancestors, named Vandehay (meaning "from the hay, from the meadow") came here from the Netherlands in the 1870s. Remington, a middle-aged woman with a whimsical smile and a glint in her eyes, is a fourth-generation herb lady. She was a war baby, born in 1943. "The GIs brought back a lot of the herbs. You go back in the magazines and you'll find very little mention of oregano. The GIs brought it back."

She wears a plain green apron and yellow plastic clogs. She sits on a little wooden bench, under the sun, and surveys her kingdom.

Her little gray house is wrapped in vines. Near it are a small barn and a greenhouse, roof darkened by Mount

St. Helens ash. The place seems a magnet for life. A sign on the greenhouse is painted with the image of a hornet. She leaves the hornets alone but warns people about them. Bees hover and spin. Barn swallows swoop and dive, making low runs through the low apple trees. The branches nearly drip with ripe fruit.

Out under the trees she keeps rows of potted herbs, with odd touches: old baby shoes and an old pair of working boots with succulents growing from them. The surrounding fields hum with insects. On the western horizon, you can see the blue foothills of the Coast Range.

A true webfoot, as native Oregonians like to call themselves, Remington grew up in Portland. Moving to this place in the country twenty-nine miles west of the city in 1973 was like coming home. This farm was owned by her grandfather's first cousin, but she did not know this when she bought it.

Her grandmother was diabetic and "a little heavy and she couldn't reach down, so I was her gatherer. I gathered the sage and rose petals and lavender and she spread the leaves and petals out to dry." She remembers the scents of childhood gathering; sometimes she has aromatic flashes, a forgotten memory of a certain plant will bring with it scenes and sounds of her grandmother moving through the fields, or standing quietly, listening beneath the trees.

"For the longest time I didn't think about why I do this, I just did it. But lately I have come to understand that, though the bank owns this land, I am here to be its steward." She and her husband, a truck driver (they have raised four children, grown and gone), now raise pheasants and let them go into the wild. Sometimes there are deer in the fields, and, rarely, elk that will lie down with the cattle at nearby farms. The Remingtons will not cultivate any of their land that floods in the spring because it is on the flyway for ducks and Canada geese.

But there is something more here for her to do. "You see, this is a birdbath. People read about me maybe in a brochure or a newspaper, and they come here from all over the world. They come and share. They're not always here at the same time, but they'll tell me something and I'll pass that on the next person who comes. I'm the birdbath."

Heavy, dark clouds move over briefly and then move on. The wind grows still, the air seems to hang heavy like an inverted bowl over this place.

I told her I was interested in the effect particular pieces of land have on people, that there are very old theories, usually among primitive cultures, that there is good land and evil land, and that people can be shaped by where they live. She was unimpressed. "It's people that do it. You can take any piece of land, and if you feed the land and don't take too much, it will give you a good life."

Some people who feel strongly about nature do not particularly like people, but she is different. Of course, the invasion of this land by people is only now beginning. Maybe it will get like rats in a maze, out-of-staters wedging into subdivisions, short-tempered people hollering at each other, freeways becoming battlegrounds, but by the time that happens here, she says maybe she'll be too blind and deaf to notice.

A weed, she says, is just a plant out of place. A petunia in a strawberry patch is a weed. In her farming methods, she grows weeds on purpose, to shade her more sensitive herbs. And she cuts the seed heads from the weeds and makes winter bouquets to feed the birds. So there is a place for weeds.

In the spring, she advertises mint socials. "The slugs are barely awake in March." People come out in the gray in their galoshes, carrying umbrellas. They talk and go away with mint pie and dried flowers, and she gives part of the profits to cancer research.

She says the baby boomers are newly attracted to herbal gardening. "Their children are off the tricycles and now they want to have a little garden." She raises white gardens and black gardens—"black pansies, blackberry lilies, black angelica"—in honor of the victims of the Vietnam War.

She smiles. "I don't sell my plants, I adopt 'em out."

The wind is picking up again. She heads for her musty storeroom/office. "Did you see the baby swallows? I don't know what kind they are, but I love 'em." The ceiling is hung with bunches of herbs and drying flowers. A spider remains untouched in its web. Her voice is musical, trilling up and down as she describes her current children: eighty-seven different lavenders, ninety-seven different geraniums, and forty-seven different mints. In the jars on the walls she keeps lemon mint, French mint, Spanish thyme, golden thyme.

On one shelf she displays lavender wands, stalks woven and pulled back, "to capture the magic of summer." Over in the corner she keeps a large jar filled with leaves and branches and seeds from all over the state. The jar is marked "Oregon." When you open it, Oregon comes out. And right now she must get back to tending her birdbath, her one true place.

Call the world, if you please, "The Vale of Soul Making." Then you will find out the use of the world.

—John Keats

Wyoming Wind

SOMETIMES YOU NEED A LITTLE EMPTINESS.

Ed Richner wrestles his jeep toward the mountains. My family and I are bouncing around on the hard seats. The jeep is chipped and dented down to its essence, like Ed himself. Pronghorn antelope race across the yellow hills. They move like a scarf caught in the wind. Here in eastern Wyoming, Ed says, "the West is still the West." Indeed. This is the ninth-largest and least populated state in America, and we're sixty miles from Casper or Rawlins, the nearest towns, half of those miles on unpaved road. By last count, only 486,185 people lived in Wyoming. That's about a fifth of the population size of the county in which I live.

Ed, sparely built, appears to be in his sixties. A rancher and a cowboy and a conservationist, his philosophy is: seek a balance; don't push anything. He explains how he sets the fences to honor the patterns of elk and antelope and deer. "That way, the wildlife doesn't take your fence down."

We move up Long Crick, stapled by beaver dams, with pools filled with eight- and ten-inch brook trout that scatter when you're twenty feet away. Later, my sons sit very still next to the water, and slowly the fish appear, but then my older boy clears his nose and the sound is like a shot; the brookies, wild electrons now, race around the pool and some of them leap out of the water in panic.

Ed drives higher. Like many Wyoming ranchers, he uses a jeep or a motorcycle to check his fences and to gather his cattle. He drives slowly on smooth tires to protect the land. He uses a motorcycle with a quiet four-cycle engine. When his cattle stray too far into the mountains he saddles a horse to go after them. Mountain lions are plentiful up in the rimrock, but they aren't much of a problem these days. In the 1930s, before Australia and other countries began to dominate the sheep market, wolves were a problem; they would slaughter fifty sheep in a night.

I ask him about the planned reintroduction of wolves to northwestern Wyoming. He shrugs. Wolves will just be one more thing to deal with. "If I can deal with drought, I can deal with wolves." Unlike some Wyoming ranchers, Ed survives drought and other natural forces by not pushing. For years he has rotated his hay harvests and the roots have held enough water in the ground.

Sometimes his cattle wander to surrounding ranches. His fellow ranchers, good neighbors, identify owner-ship by the red clips in their ears, and they care for the cattle until Ed comes to get them. He returns the favor. But one nearby ranch is owned by a bank that hires transient hands. "I go over there and find my steers in their corral and I ask the hands when the cattle were fed or watered and they say, 'Oh, a couple weeks ago.'" Banks push.

Right now, he points: Up on a ridge where the mountain sheep live is the dark shape of one of his steers. "People think they don't climb." He smiles and drives on, watching the fence for breaks, leaning forward to look for tracks in the ruts ahead.

In a dip between two hills, he stops the jeep. We can only hear the wind. He gets out and slides his baseball cap back on his forehead. He leads us to a teepee ring, three concentric circles of stones that once anchored hides. He estimates that this ring dates to the 1860s. From it, we can see far across the plains. We turn and look behind us at the curve of horizon and see one, then two, then three antelope, watching us.

Ed talks about how hard it must have been for the homesteaders here, walking down to the river, before the dams kept it from freezing, to carve out blocks of ice in the endless winters. It still is hard. Ed has built snow fences around his land, one of them shaped like the prow of a ship, and as large as a ship, where his cattle huddle.

"Sometimes the snow builds up in drifts," he says, "and then the wind comes and blows the dry snow, and even though no snow falls from the clouds, a blizzard will blow for a week."

Across Wyoming, independent ranchers are a dying breed. Cowboys are riding their motorcycles into the sunset. But Ed hangs on. "You've got to diversify," he says. He's got his rental cabins. He's got his 200 head of cattle. Someday, he and his wife may move on, but for now, they've got it all.

We're parked on an 8,000-foot peak now, watching the afternoon thunderheads approach. The plains below and the sky above are like the palms of outstretched hands. These hands can close suddenly into fists, and they are beginning to do that now. So Ed heads back down the mountain. He pushes it. We hang onto our hats, laughing, and he races the lightning home.

That night everyone is asleep in the cabin, but I can hear my older son stirring. I get him up and take him outside and tell him, "This may be the only time in your life that you'll see the Milky Way and lightning at the same time." We stand there shivering. My arm is around his shoulders.

We listen to the coyotes and the thunder and watch the lightning over the mountains and we look up at the spinning stars.

Eating Trout

THE BIG TROUT MOVED THROUGH the clear water and weeds. It disappeared. It came back. This was the kind of moment that small boys, and their fathers, dream of. Matthew hung over the rail, his little feet planted far apart, his shoulders scrunched up with anticipation.

The moral ambiguities of life are never more evident than when dealing with an eight year old. For example, in the past, I have had to patiently explain to Matthew the virtues of catching and releasing fish. Matthew has had some trouble understanding this policy. He has lobbied for a different approach—to take them home to show his Mom.

This time, he would have a different attitude.

The fish grabbed the worm and headed south. Matthew pulled north, but the fish slipped away and vanished. Two other boys, older than Matthew, threw their bait toward where the fish had been. "Maybe you guys should try the other side of the dock," Matthew said to them. "I'll bet that fish is over there."

I arched an eyebrow and looked at my son. The older boys knew an artificial lure when they saw one; they moved their rods closer to his. We waited for the big fish to return. After a while, Matthew announced, "Dad, I've got to pee."

"How badly?" I asked.

"It can wait," he said, looking at the water.

Then the trout, with the persistence of Jaws, swooped back into view, tapped each boy's worm, and settled on Matthew's. "Wait, Matthew ... let him take it ... let him ... NOW," I cried, and Matthew set the hook like a pro. The trout took off; Matthew's rod arched. The older boys cheered. Fishermen from the other end of the dock ran toward us.

Nikon in hand, I waved and hooted to my wife, who was sitting warm in the Volkswagen; she leapt from the van, believing, of course, that the worst had happened, that her son had fallen in and disappeared and would never be seen again, or something like that. She came running, hair flying.

By now, the fish was on the dock. People were congratulating Matthew, whose knees were visibly shaking. "Whew!" he said. "When I get home, I'll have to have a victory pee." Then he asked, "Are we going to let it go?"

"No, not this one. He's bleeding and won't make it. We'll have to eat him."

I slipped the trout into a plastic bag. The light was fading. Matthew and his mother headed back to the van with the fish. My wife does not fish. She carries spiders from the house. But she is a good sport.

I finished packing up the gear. As I approached the van, I knew something was wrong, knew it from the way my wife, in silhouette, was looking at Matthew. She looked at me sadly. He was holding the slimy bag and tears were sliding down his cheeks.

"He wanted to let it go," she said.

The victory had slipped away. Now a new consciousness

and morality was flooding his heart. A forty-six year old heart is better at rationalizing.

"Well, look, let me see if it's still alive," I said, knowing better but hoping for a way out. I took the trout to the edge of the lake, removed it from the bag, knelt down, cradled it in my hands, and moved it back and forth in the water. Blood flowed from its gills into the weeds. The fish was stiff.

My wife's shadow appeared on the water.

"Maybe I should just leave it here," I said to her. I looked back at the van, where Matthew's head was still bowed.

"You shouldn't lie to him," she said.

I returned the fish to the bag and walked back to the van. "Did he eat lunch before we left home?" I asked her, implying that was the reason he had cried.

On the way home, I thought about how the trout had come back again and again. Even a house fly can take on a personality if you swat at it long enough, and when you smash it, the familiarity can breed a little grief.

I thought, too, of how many fish I had thoughtlessly killed as a boy, buckets of them not even eaten, but dumped into holes in the garden. Both my sons had more compassionate responses to killing their first fish. Both wept.

At home, I put the fish in the sink and asked Matthew if he wanted to help me clean it. "No!" he said, and headed for the bathroom.

His mother made him a bowl of Franco-American Shnookums & Meat. He sat at the table and ate, and I talked to him about fishing and eating.

I told him that this fish had eaten smaller fish to survive. This was probably not helpful. An eight year old would probably deduce from this that a larger animal, then, is supposed to eat him.

"It's important to understand," I continued, getting in deeper, "that the animals we eat aren't born packaged. It's important to understand the whole process."

"Well, if you know 'bout that, maybe you won't want to eat animals at all," he said, firmly.

I looked at him. "Let's weigh your fish," I said.

I got the scale out. "I'll bet it's two pounds." I said.

"Pound and a half," he said.

I held it up. "You're right, Matthew."

"Can I hold it?" he asked. "Sure." I put it into the sink, filled with water, and he moved his hands along its sides and smiled.

My wife made a sauce and cooked the fish and I lit candles and we sat at the table. Matthew watched us eat. He did not eat any of the trout, but he was feeling better and so were we. He was glad we liked his fish.

Life gives life. And moves on.

The Strand
of Time

In small villages, people possess the most
precious thing there is—time.

> —Santiago Chavez, an artist raised
> in Puerto de Luna, New Mexico

The Door of the Moon

THE KNEE-HIGH PILE OF ASTONISHINGLY RED CHILES was heaped up in front of an old television on the floor of the porch. The old man, Jose Padilla, was ushering visitors into the adobe house and scooping chiles into paper bags.

Some of the visitors sat down on folding chairs. Jose's widowed sister-in-law brought out bowls of sliced watermelon. This is a yearly ritual in Puerto de Luna—the "door of the moon"—where the old year is ushered out by the chile harvest, and the new year is welcomed with the spring planting, and everything in between is waiting. People drive here from cities and towns hundreds of miles away for the chile, which is good in itself, but the conversation is better—because during this ritual, the years bleed together.

Boni Lucero, for instance, was talking about the year 1906.

"Six years old when I came here." He spat a watermelon seed into the communal bucket. "Celso Baca had all the land around here then. Why, he even had buggies with rubber tires. Had this big hacienda in Santa Rosa. Celso Baca came here right from Spain. He wore a big stovepipe hat and a cape. Oh, he was an aristocrat! He had a lot of burros. Every kid who moved to town, he gave them a burro. He gave me one, had long hair. Threw me off."

Another seed hit the bucket.

"That hacienda, it's the mortuary now."

Outside, Jose Padilla was bringing another basket of chiles up from the fields. A pickup roared up, packed with an Albuquerque family. A burly father, who only yesterday had been a boy in this valley, jumped out of the truck and hugged Padilla, small and bent and embarrassed. The young man's T-shirt was emblazoned with the word "Korea." He was laughing.

"See, I came all the way from Korea."

This ritual homecoming continues, even as so many of the vacant adobe houses dissolve back into the mud, or disappear into the wind.

The Pecos River, shallow and wide, runs through here and so the valley is always green. Up in northern New Mexico, near Santa Fe, similar Hispanic farm valleys are being subdivided for wealthy Californians and New Yorkers looking for spiritual salvation and good investment returns. But Puerto de Luna is still far from anything chic; there's not a soy burger within a hundred miles. About the only tourist attraction is a peculiar lake in nearby Santa Rosa. Shaped like an elevator shaft, the water is so deep and clear that divers come from all around the country to sit on the bottom at night and look up at the stars.

Fewer than a hundred people live here today, but the valley's little civilization stretches back a long way. Hispanics in New Mexico do not call themselves Mexican-American; they call themselves "Spanish." So it is in Puerto de Luna. In 1541, searching for the seven cities of Cibola, Coronado halted his army here and built a bridge of logs across the Pecos. In the mid-1800s, when the village was the Sumner County seat, a thousand people lived here. One night, Billy the Kid was held at the local jail, and he broke out, killing two men. People here seem to have a vague admiration for him, because he was willing to do anything to survive.

Penitentes still live in the area. An ancient Catholic offshoot, Penitentes are self-flagellators, disavowed by the church. A few of them still meet in hidden adobe chapels on holy week to "crucify" an honored member, hanging him from a cross with leather thongs. Until the 1930s, in some parts of New Mexico, nails were used. The Penitentes survive, but they are not an important part of the culture anymore.

What is important is the ring of red-rock mesas; and the preciousness of water; and the spring wind that comes through the gap at the end of the valley and shakes the cottonwoods; and the ristras, the scarlet strings of dried chiles that hang on the sides of the adobe houses, marking good years. Boni Lucero can remember bad years, in 1917 and 1930, when the cattle market dried up and families killed their cows. Those years were marked not with ristras, but with clotheslines of drying jerky.

And of course the homecomings are important.

In the kitchen, Jose's sister-in-law, Rita Padilla, was rolling a crust for an apple pie. Her sons, Andy and Juan, both in their twenties, were sitting at the table. Rita pointed at them with her knife.

"They should stay," she said sharply. "They are the future. I've been working on them, I'm trying to train them. To me, this is a great life. Keeps people young. You can think here. Raise your own food, your own meat. You need a side job; that's what my husband did." She pointed at her sons. "They could turn this place into a paradise. We need young people. Retired people can't do anything."

Andy grinned. Juan got up suddenly without saying anything and went into the next room to watch a football game.

That night, after the homecoming was over, Rita's youngest son, Michael (who is fourteen and may be the last Padilla to be raised in the valley), and old Jose Padilla walked over to a house where nobody lives. There is a rough-hewn beam in this house salvaged from the jail that held Billy the Kid. The family that had lived there had moved away six months before. A visitor was staying there that night. The three of them sat at a table, under the old beam.

"I read a story about Billy the Kid once, and I said, this is bull," said Jose. "My mother said Billy the Kid didn't bother nobody but I don't know much about that."

He was turning a Bic lighter over and over in his hand. He began to talk about the irrigation ditch. For a long time, Jose had been a "ditch rider" who cleaned out the ditch and kept it going. Jose had never married; the ditch, in a way, was his wife. The ditch has been married before; maintained by loving hands, it has functioned without fail for at least a hundred years.

"It was an old ditch when I came here. They made it work with shovels and horses and mules. The dam for it was made with sabinos, cedar trees and brush and rocks, laying these on one layer at a time. No engineers leveled it. No nothing." He laughed and then looked directly at the visitor. "You think you can do that?"

Then he looked away and turned the lighter.

"I wish we had more people. I wish they didn't quit."

The visitor asked, "Will there be anybody here in fifty years?"

He shook his head and looked at the lighter and didn't look up for a long time. And then he was up and out of the house, walking home along the dirt road with the visitor and Michael, who scooted along, pushing his bicycle with his feet, watching his uncle with admiration. They passed one of the valley's old cemeteries with its little white crosses all askew.

"He wants to die here," said Michael.

"And be buried in that cemetery?" asked the visitor.

"No, all his relatives are in the one across the river."

Suddenly Jose turned and lifted his arms up and down. "Look at that," he said, smiling. The full moon, like a face, was hanging there above the gap.

The door of the moon.

If only I could push my fist into the cold current of time, and then open my hand, and feel it thread through my fingers. If only I could hold it. Sometimes this almost seems possible. During moments of clarity, I realize that I belong in my time, that I am married to whom I am married, that my children are my children, that my family of origin is my one and only original family, and that this is my time. I do not know why these moments are so startling. Perhaps it's because I spend so much time thinking about alternatives. If only I were a different height, smarter, had better hair; if only I lived in New Mexico, or New York, anywhere other than the suburban stucco wastelands. If only I were younger, older, had been born in the nineteenth century; if only I could be around when human beings leave this solar system, when they travel to the stars. If only.

When I was three or four I was struck with a thought that stopped me in my tracks. I was walking through fallen pears on my grandmother's half acre. Their smell was full and tart in the top of my nose. I stopped and looked at the pear tree and the little corpses around it, and suddenly knew that I had come into this body, like everyone else into theirs, through the crown of my head, like a stream of sparkling dust. I still believe it is true, as true as only a dream can be. What stopped me in my tracks was not the realization that I had been dropped into my body. What stopped me was the question why. Why, I wondered, had I been dropped into this body, instead of that one, or that one, or any other? I did not mind being in this body. But why this body? Why this time?

Many years went by. Hours before my mother's heart slowed like a clock running down, I held her rigid hand and looked at her eyes which were stilled like glazed fruit, and suddenly saw —or felt?—a shooting upward, from out of her, near her eyes, that same kind of stardust. Later, I walked outside in the darkness and saw a halo of fine rain around a parking lot light; the water seemed frozen in time.

Now, as I remember that rain, I'm sitting in a window seat of McDonald's, watching the passersby, and I wonder again why I am in the time in which I am. As I grow older, the puzzlement is giving way to acceptance or gratitude. This is my body. This is my time. Even this booth at McDonald's is mine, for now. Knowing this—and I do not know it all the time—gives me focus, makes me value my family and friends and my own senses and the fragile strands that hold us in place, before they let us go, all the more.

Haunted Houses

THERE ARE SUCH THINGS AS HAUNTED HOUSES, or, more accurately, houses that haunt us. Houses can be time-markers or time machines. They connect us to past selves and loved ones gone or changed.

A woman came to our door last Sunday. She said she had grown up in our house. My wife invited her in and gave her a tour of the house. She said it had not changed much since she had lived there.

"Those tiles," she said. "I had forgotten those tiles."

We traded notes about the back patio wall, which moves an inch every spring when the rains come. She said the wall was moving when she was a little girl. Standing outside on the lawn, she looked at the house, and was silent for a while. Her eyes were a bit sad.

"Does it seem different to you?" I asked.

"It seems smaller."

This quiet woman with the long-ago look in her eyes said that she had been glad when she heard that a writer and his family had bought the house, because her father was a writer (I work in the same study today) and because children would grow up in the house, as she had.

She said she sometimes fantasized about buying the house herself, but she lives in San Francisco, and that would be impractical.

Later, this set me to thinking. The rich are different from you and me: They can buy the houses that haunt them.

Ross Perot bought his boyhood home in Texarkana and preserved it. The bricks of his home, in his absence, had been painted white, so he asked that they be sandblasted. The sandblasting did not work, so he ordered the house torn apart and the bricks turned around so that their unpainted sides faced outward. Dolly Parton bought her childhood home. "That's where I take my retreats and write my songs," she says. Bill Clinton has yet to buy his past. His childhood home, haunted by alcohol and abuse, is a burnt-out hulk.

I wonder if baby boomers will be particularly susceptible to the fantasy of buying their childhood homes.

Pioneering generations were concerned with moving on. Unless they are legends in their own minds or times (as is Perot, take your pick), most of the people I know in their sixties express little nostalgia for the houses of their childhood. For my parents, who were members of the Jetsons Generation, Victorian was gauche, contemporary was in. They yearned for the new; they believed in the future.

Today, we're less hopeful and more transient than our parents; a house is less a home than an investment. If our childhood houses haunt us more, perhaps that is why.

In the future, as home ownership diminishes, perhaps gadgets and furniture will be more haunted than houses. At a recent family reunion, my wife asked her younger brother how he felt when he saw his father's old tools in a new garage. Their parents had moved from California to a senior housing complex in Oregon.

He looked at his father's table saw for a long time,

and said, "Whenever I look at this saw, I remember standing next to him for hours, and how the sawdust matted in the hair of his arms." My grandmother's house in Independence, Missouri, where I spent part of my childhood, is down the street from Harry and Bess Truman's house. The neighborhood, and my grandmother's house, which was built in 1889, are filled with apocryphal ghosts: Jesse James hid out down the street; Truman is said to have given his first speech from the front porch. My relatives sat on that porch one night listening to the cicadas sing, and in the twilight watched Uncle Tommy walk up the sidewalk toward them at the precise time he was killed, several miles away, in an automobile accident.

A few weeks ago, I took my mother back to Independence to be buried, and I visited the house, which I have fantasized about buying. The radiators had been ripped from it and were stacked nearby; it had been gutted like a fish and the porch was rotting away.

I do not think I will visit it again.

On Sunday, I told the woman who had come to our door that she could come back anytime and see her house, come inside and touch the tiles and see if the wall had moved some more.

Moving Our Memories

A FEW DAYS AFTER WE MOVED TO OUR NEW HOME, we found ourselves grieving for the old one. Matthew, so small then, came up with a solution. "We should sell this house, and rent it to somebody," he said, meaning the house we had just bought. "Then we should buy our old house and move back in."

My wife and I explained that we could not buy our old house back. He thought for a while and came up with Plan B. "Here's what we'll do," he said, matter-of-factly. "We'll go back to our old house and . . . you know that little door in the door?" He was describing the brass peephole that opened like a miniature door. "We'll go up to that little door," he continued, "and we'll push it open and we'll suck all of our memories out and bring them back to our new house."

My wife and I considered Plan B. It did sound like a good idea.

According to our older son, Jason, the problem with our new house was that it had no memories in it, at least not our memories. He was right. The wallpaper was not colored with our lives. The carpet had not soaked up the particular sounds of our children's tennis shoes. (The good news was that it had not yet soaked up the smell of our dog, either.)

My wife, who is no New Age faddist, has a theory about houses, that they absorb the memories of the people who have lived in them. She felt this was particularly true about our old house, the one we had just left. I am sure there were good times in that house before we moved there, but the stories we learned about it from neighbors were for the most part tragic. A marriage had dissolved in that old house, a woman had died there from a long illness, and below it, in the canyon, there was a huge eucalyptus tree from which, years before, a child had fallen and been paralyzed. He spent the rest of his childhood looking down into the canyon and at the tree from the screened-in porch where he sat.

During the years we lived in that house, we had compensated for and, perhaps, overcome its past. Shortly after we moved into the old house, the old tree died and the canyon filled with the sounds of our boys. In my office in the converted garage, I wrote many columns and three books, often with my sons scrawling with crayons or tapping on their computer at the desk next to mine. In the main house, the walls were christened with crayon scribbles.

Slowly the sadness from the prior owners faded, and our residue settled on the walls. Still, there were no children in the neighborhood for our kids to play with, and we lived on a fast street, and the house was far too small for a growing family. So we moved.

We never went back to open the little door to suck our memories out, but we did begin to fill the walls of our new home. It was more of a blank slate than the old one had been.

The first task was to transport some old memories to these walls.

One of the good things about moving to a larger house is that it has more wall space, so we pulled out photographs that had been stashed under the beds and hung them. And my wife bought several matted picture frames to hold multiple family snapshots.

We reached further back. We drove to our rented storage unit, a kind of U-Haul mausoleum, where my mother's prized possessions are stored, and sweating in the stifling heat, we went through a few boxes and looked for pieces of the past. I pulled out a colorful, ornate studio shot of my mother when she was four or five, and my wife silently shook her head. It was too soon after her death, and the photo filled us with too much emotion.

Deep in the unit I found a large oval photograph of my grandmother, taken near the turn of the century. She is wearing a high, laced collar, and her hair is piled on her head, which is tilted to one side. She seems to be looking into the past and into the future and deep into herself. Her eyes are filled with the kindness that I remember. We took the photograph to the new house and hung it above the fireplace, and suddenly the living room, which had been someone else's until that moment, filled with her love and ours, too. Suddenly we were home.

"It's nice having her there," said my wife. "It's a way to have your mother on the wall without feeling so sad. I can see your mother in her eyes." Now we had more of the past with us than in the old house. Our older son suggested the next step. "We've got to make some new memories to fill the house," he said.

And this happened faster than we would have imagined.

The boys have more freedom and friends in the new neighborhood than they did in the old one. In our cul-de-sac, Jason and his new friends do endless circles on their bikes; Matthew has adopted the neighbors next door as surrogate grandparents. Children rush in and out of the house, and the walls reverberate with their calls and whispers, and my grandmother smiles down on all of this.

The Ultimate Go-Cart

SOMETIMES, WITH YOUR OWN CHILDREN, you may suddenly feel that you are a visitor to their time, that your true home is in the past. This is not a comforting thought, but what is even more disconcerting is when you feel the past begin to let go of you.

"Do you still have family ties in Kansas City?" a friend asked recently. "No," I said, "they're all gone."

I was startled by my answer: All gone.

I had not been back to Kansas City in a year and a half, when my brother and I took our mother home. We transported her in a coffin in the cargo hold of a Boeing 727.

On the plane, my brother and I had a terrific argument; demons from the past flew through the cabin. I believe now it was our anger at being left alone, at being forced to recognize our adulthood, because now both our parents were gone.

Funny the way things go: When you are a child you yearn to become an adult; when you finally become one, you wish that you could be told a story.

We had a day's wait before the burial, so we rented a car and a motel room near one of our boyhood homes, which is on a little lake. And that afternoon we went fishing in our mother's honor.

In our family, the best times were spent fishing. That day, as the stiff wind came across the lake, it blew away some of our anger. We remembered our mother as we made long casts, side by side.

The next day, we drove to the cemetery and followed the wrong hearse and ended up at what looked like a Mafia funeral. This was how things usually went in our family, and my mother would have enjoyed the humor of the moment.

Somehow, we found the right spot and we met the two other people who had come, my mother's childhood girlfriend and my mother's thoughtful cousin Tommy, now in his seventies, who had flown up from San Antonio.

After we said a few words at the graveside, we shared some awkward moments. We began to walk away. My brother turned and went back and opened the casket and dropped his commercial fishing license into it. He was crying.

As part of our memorial, we followed Tommy to my grandmother's house in Independence. It was built by our great-grandparents in 1889, and a book still sold at the nearby Truman Library praises it for its "gables, the turned columns with elaborate brackets, and the band of fish-scale shingles."

We stood outside and looked at the old steam radiators stacked like skeletons in the brown grass; at the stumps of the grand old elms on which choruses of cicadas sang on summer nights long ago; at the crumbling porch on which Tom and my mother played, and from which, wearing a Superman cape my mother made, I jumped.

It was a dead house now; it looked as if someone was preparing it to be razed. The temperature had plummeted. I looked over at Tommy. He was shivering, shoulders bunched up, eyes filled with tears.

I decided then that I would not return to the old family home again, perhaps not even to Kansas City. But just when you think the past has let go of you, and you have resigned yourself to adulthood, time folds back.

Not long ago, I was back in Kansas City, asked by an organization to come and give a speech on the new landscape of childhood and family life. There had been a little story in the Kansas City Star mentioning the speech. Turnout was less than the organizers had hoped for, but when I arrived I was told someone special was waiting for me.

It was Dr. Unruh, my junior high principal, whom I had not seen in thirty years. I had mentioned him briefly in a column, and someone sent it to him. He wrote me, saying I must have been one of the good kids, because he didn't remember me.

I wrote him back and reminded him that he had suspended me from school for a variety of sins, and his sermon (he looked like Daddy Warbucks) had impressed me: "You're a talented kid, but you've got to learn to do one thing and do it right. You're outta here!"

In the speech, I told the story of the lasting effect he had had on me and how those words still come back to me when I am trying to do too much.

Other people from the past had also come: Gerry Hollembeak, my high school history teacher, two high school girlfriends, and a woman who introduced herself as the sister of Bill Irwin, a childhood friend. She said he had wanted to come, but was home with the flu and she had come in his place.

I had not seen or spoken to Bill in thirty-five years. He had been the oldest and the coolest kid on the block. He had a jelly-roll haircut, with wings on the side, a ducktail in back, crew cut on top with a waterfall in front.

I had been the shrimp on the block, and he had taken it upon himself to protect me. I remember looking up from a dog pile of kids to see bodies flying and Billy swinging one of them around by the feet.

Billy had also, in a paternal way, picked me—me!—as his partner to build a go-cart. This was in the days when boys competed to see who could build the best go-cart, which usually consisted of a plank of wood, two axles, four wheels, and a rope to steer with. All the kids in the neighborhood knew that once Billy Irwin put his mind to it, he would build the Ultimate Go-Cart.

He and I worked on it for weeks in his basement. The great day came, and we hauled the Ultimate Go-Cart up to the hill. The awe-struck kids, including my brother, lined the street in anticipation.

The machine was equipped with an elaborate seat, a steering wheel, a dashboard. It was heavy, four feet wide and five feet long, and probably had fins.

Billy pushed me off and the cart gathered speed. The wheels wailed, my hair flew, kids cheered. I reached the place where we always turned off and leaned into the steering wheel and ... the right front wheel bit into wood. The axle was too short! The cart and I hurtled into a ditch.

The kids wandered off. Billy and I hauled the thing to my back yard. We never mentioned or rode the Ultimate Go-Cart again.

After my speech, Billy's sister told me that after their parents were gone he had moved back to their house on that street.

The next day, I visited my mother's grave. The sod line was still visible. The weather was good. I came home to San Diego and told my sons the story of Billy Irwin and the Ultimate Go-Cart, and their eyes grew wide.

If someone asks me again if I still have family ties in Kansas City, I am not sure how I will answer.

When we raise our children, we relive our childhoods. Forgotten memories, painful and pleasurable, rise to the surface. A lost ball recalls another lost ball, twenty, thirty years ago; the smell of cedar brings forth the Christmas of 1957; the burial of a hamster brings forth tears of another time for another pet—perhaps a turtle wrapped in tissue and buried beneath an elm tree. When we hear ourselves raise our voices at our children, or see or hear ourselves through their eyes and ears, we meet the ghosts of our own young parents. So each of us thinks, almost daily, of how our own childhood compares with our children's, and of what our children's future will hold.

First Love

JASON AND I WERE SITTING IN HIS ROOM, on the bed between the geckos and the bullfrogs. He was twelve. "Did I ever tell you about Cecilia Nichols?" I asked.

"No," he answered. He said this in the tone he uses when he knows a story is coming. Most of the time, he enjoys these stories. Jason is in the sixth grade. We were in his new room, in the new neighborhood, and we were talking about how difficult a move can be.

"When I was your age, my family moved, too," I said.

That move, in 1960, had been difficult. One reason was that I had to leave Cecilia Nichols behind.

"Is she the one in the picture?" asked Jason.

"Yep."

A year or so before my mother died, she sent a box of memorabilia from our family's early days. In the box was an autograph book from Southwood Elementary, Raytown, Missouri, 1958. I had pasted only one photograph in the book. It was of Cecilia, who glowed in the picture, just as she does in my memory.

Cecilia was my secret. She was one of those rare people loved by teachers as well as students. I remember, in second grade, sliding down the hall on my coat to get her attention. And, later, passing notes back and forth, those geometric puzzles with special messages hidden beneath each folded corner.

Once, at recess, I saw Cecilia sitting on the asphalt

191

with a group of her girlfriends. I ran past and shot a hard spit wad at her. To my horror, the spit wad smacked her, with a loud report, in the middle of her forehead. She burst into tears. I ran away.

"Did she ever forgive you?" Jason asked.

"The next day, she handed me a note. It said that if I respected her, I would stay away from her." I stayed away for three months. At recess, I would watch her from a distance. I was Zorro, incognito, protecting her from the shadows. Then one day she handed me another note, and I came in from the cold.

As adults, we can underestimate or discount our children's emotional attachments, partly because our children are likely to keep them secret. Telling this story to my son was an indirect way of acknowledging this, between the geckos and the bullfrogs.

"In sixth grade," I told him, "the school district divided Southwood's students and sent some of us off to a new elementary school. I pined for Cecilia."

The following summer, I gathered my courage and rode my bicycle across a highway and miles beyond my boundary.

I found Cecilia's small white house. In the glaring sunlight, I walked up to the door and knocked. She came to the door. I could barely see her behind the screen, but when my eyes adjusted, I suddenly realized that she had grown much taller than I.

My courage fled. I jumped on my bike and rode away.

Shortly afterward my family moved across the state line, which, at that time, felt like moving to another galaxy, and though I told no one—especially my parents—my heart ached for years. I thought it would never heal.

"Did you ever see her again?" asked Jason. The light was fading in his room.

"At a regional junior high band concert, I sat behind her. I played the cornet. She played saxophone. I sucked in my cheeks to look cool. She never saw me."

But a few years later, I was picked as the ninth grade exchange student to Raytown South High School, Cecilia's school unless she, too, had moved. The visit filled me with anticipation and dread. Over three days at the vast Raytown South, I kept hearing stories about her, how Cecilia Nichols was the smartest kid in school, but everyone loved her anyway.

On the last day, the exchange students were introduced at the school assembly. We were paraded across the stage. Late that afternoon, after most of the school buses had come and gone, I waited with the other exchange students for our ride back to Kansas. I felt empty. I had blown my last chance.

Then from down an empty hall I heard running footsteps. They grew louder. And Cecilia rounded the corner and ran up to me.

I was taller than she now.

She was out of breath, and she said, "I was hoping you hadn't left. I remember you."

We stood close and made small talk. Then my ride came. That was the last time I saw her. But it didn't matter. As the car pulled away I felt wonderful, and complete.

Stories have a way of ending the way they're meant to end.

I looked at Jason. Hands behind his head, he was staring into space. Both of us were smiling.

>>>>

I tell you that I have a long way to go before I am where one begins.... You are so young, so before all beginnings, and I want to beg you, as much as I can, to be patient toward all that is unsolved in your heart and to try to love the questions themselves like locked rooms and like books that are written in a very foreign tongue. Do not now seek the answers, which cannot be given you because you would not be able to live them. And the point is, to live everything. Live the questions now. Perhaps you will then gradually, without noticing it, live along some distant day into the answer.

Resolve to be always beginning—to be a beginner!

—Rainer Maria Rilke

The Virtual Ghost

O thou, the early author of my blood,
Whose youthful spirit, in me regenerate.
Doth with his lofty and shrill-sounding throat
Awake the snorting like a horse.

> —Text generated by artificial intelligence, from
> what University of California computer scientists call
> "the Shakespeare corpus."

SOMETIMES WORLDS CONVERGE, explode and create a new one. Lately, I have been wondering what will happen when the worlds of high definition television (or, better yet, the three-dimensional hologram), digital sound, artificial intelligence, and theories of virtual reality converge with the yearnings of the human heart. Here is one possibility: the virtual ghost.

This notion first appeared to me (an apparition!) after interviewing a series of cutting-edge technophiles and thinkers, including Byron Reeves, a professor of communications at Stanford, one of the few people in the country studying how enhanced images are processed by the human mind.

Reeves suggests that the power of highly realistic electronic images may be even greater than we know. His studies, which have focused on relatively low-tech media, show that if you look at an old black-and-white photo of your mother or anyone else you have known, subconsciously you will react to it physiologically, "almost identically as you would if the person were standing in front of you." Add sound and motion to the image, says Reeves, and your "reactions are all the more complete."

So what happens when we add newly available and evolving technological wizardry? Here enters—with a click and a hum—the virtual ghost.

Imagine this. You'll be able to bring back the dead. Kind of.

Already, cryogenics companies around California will freeze Grandma's head. Why not digitize her instead? In the future, Grandma or Dad or Mom or anyone else who wants to leave behind a special legacy, if not their legs, will drive over to Virtual Ghost, Inc. (an imaginary company, so far).

The company techs will record and store Mom's image and the sound and patterns of her voice, in digital form. Using an artificial intelligence program, the company techs will ask her a long series of questions; in this way, her favorite phrases, life history, and family stories (including some that she has never told) will be preserved. The program also will record Mom's thought patterns, her logic, the predictability—or unpredictability—of her emotions.

Mom dies, but her virtual ghost remains. From that point on, her relatives and descendants can sit on the family room couch, slip on a virtual reality helmet, and ask Mom questions, hold extended conversations with her on just about any topic, including the wounds that went unspoken in life.

Setting aside, for a moment, the creepiness of this

idea, I called Robert Hecht-Nielsen, chair of the board of HNC Inc., a San Diego company specializing in artificial intelligence software. Hecht-Nielsen is one of the country's leading experts on neural networks, the branch of artificial intelligence that allows a computer to learn on its own when fed raw data.

"If you just wanted an image that moved and did not speak, that could be done today," he said. "Using existing technology, you could also carry on a dialogue with it." Though the apparition's intelligence level would not be high, it would express itself with some of Mom's idiosyncrasies intact.

I asked Hecht-Nielsen when he thought science will be able to create a full-fledged, 3-D, conversational virtual ghost who could think as Mom might have thought.

"One that would be convincing to a child, I'd say in three or four decades," said Hecht-Nielsen. "But it might take hundreds of years to create one that adults could turn to for advice."

Maybe, but he may be overestimating our needs. Adults use Ouija boards to ask advice from the dead. In any case, assuming a few major breakthroughs, virtual ghosts might be lurking around the corner.

The possibility raises questions.

Would your conversation with Virtual Mom be fundamentally different from the one you have, daily, in your own head?

Could she be programmed to age as she might have in real life?

Could we, at some point, pour everything that Lincoln

wrote into a neural network, digitize all the photographs ever taken of him, and produce a Virtual Abe? (Scientists might compensate for unknown information by adding cultural detail from Lincoln's time, just as frog DNA was used to fill out the missing pieces of dinosaur DNA in *Jurassic Park*.) Could a virtual meeting of virtual ghosts be arranged? For example, could the Pentagon bring Lincoln, Napoleon, and Janis Joplin together for an evening of music and military strategizing?

Hecht-Nielsen says that bringing back the famously dead is already trendy in academe. After we spoke, he faxed me the above stanzas of faux-Shakespeare; these were created by pouring the Bard's work into a computer and asking it to produce a new work. Similar programs have composed music that Bach might have produced had he lived three extra centuries.

Meanwhile, back to Mom, now preserved in silicon or some other magic sand of the future. If you could speak to her virtual ghost, what would you ask? What would she say? What would you hear in your heart?

In the early morning hours, when you cannot sleep; when you're staring into the refrigerator; when you're on the tennis court; when you're meeting with your boss; when you're lying on the living room floor with your child climbing across your chest, what are the internal questions you ask yourself about growing older? And when do those questions begin? In your twenties, your thirties, your forties? Does time run out? Do we fall from the web?

The internal questions we ask ourselves about aging are almost always negative or, at best, maintenance questions. As we pass forty, we tend to ask questions such as: How can I keep from falling behind in the workplace? How can I maintain my sexuality? How can I stay healthy? How can I keep my children from slipping away as they grow? And so on. The answers of aging lie in the nature of the questions. Change the nature of the questions, and everything is transformed.

Found Time

WE HAVE MORE TIME THAN WE SUSPECT. Not long ago, Jack Levine, Florida's leading child advocate, stood before the partners and associates of a major Miami law firm and asked them to give up some time—spectator time. Like many Americans, Levine is troubled by the fact that nobody seems to have much time anymore to build community, to volunteer in the schools or join a service club or even to know their neighbors.

"There are three essential divisions in our waking hours: work, leisure, and family time," Levine told the lawyers. "So if we're going to spend more time building community, where is that time going to come from?"

Probably not from work, not in this economy. Certainly not from family; we don't have enough family time now. What about leisure? Depending on which survey you trust, leisure time is shrinking, too.

Nonetheless, Levine believes that big chunks of leisure time can be redirected to family and community. "For too many Americans today, leisure is defined as the first six-pack in the second quarter of the second TV football game," he says. "We've equated leisure with spectatorism, to the detriment of our kids, our communities, our economy. "We've got to say to ourselves that time with family and time with community are forms of true leisure. We've got to carve away some of the spectatorism in our lives."

Well, wait: I want my PBS, and the *X-Files*, too. A friend says, "Watching TV alone is a relief. It's the only time I don't have to be a person who acts a certain way." I can relate. On the other hand, I remember my grandmother and the men and women of her generation, how they relaxed by doing, by making, by socializing. And I recall how fulfilled they seemed when they did that.

Some experts believe that the true goal of leisure should be fulfillment, not gratification: that it should have the same intensity as good work. Not everyone would agree with that definition, but this is true: more and more, we like to watch.

In 1985, Americans watched TV about fifteen hours a week, 40 percent of their free time, twice as much time as they spent "visiting," the second most common leisure activity. Today, the average college student watches twenty-one hours of TV per week, according to one study. The truth is, we don't even know how many hours we spend watching now that TV's saturate schools, malls, hospitals, restaurants, doctors offices, airports, and airplanes.

Jim Spring of Leisure Trends, an adjunct to The Gallup Organization, puts leisure time into three categories: No-brainers, brainers, and puzzlers. No-brainers, such as watching TV, are passive spectator activities. Brainers include socializing and other forms of leisure that actually demand some thinking and interaction. And puzzlers include such activities as fishing and skiing, Spring reports in *American Demographics* magazine.

"Television viewing is such a perfect no-brainer, that many people don't remember doing it at all," he says.

When asked: "What did you do yesterday in your leisure time?" only 31 percent of one study's respondents mentioned television. But 77 percent 'fessed up when they were asked the more direct question: "Did you watch television yesterday?"

Though Americans spend an increasing amount of leisure time on no-brainers, Spring reports that people actually prefer brainers and puzzlers. He also describes "the large difference between expectation and reality." When he did a study for the alpine ski industry, Spring found that "in any given year, as few as 65 percent of self-described skiers actually go skiing ... Many people who consider themselves skiers have not skied at all in the last four to five years. One self-proclaimed skier had not skied since 1947!"

Meanwhile, according to the National Center for Health Statistics, participation in exercise and strenuous leisure activity began to decline in the mid-'80s.

If people are jogging less, it's doubtful that they'll go to community meetings more. But maybe Jack Levine is on to something when he suggests that we have more time than we think we do, for community, friends, and family. Recently, four governors urged their states' schools, libraries, cities, civic groups, and families to declare a "TV Turnoff Week." As alternatives, citizens were offered free workshops, magic shows, swimming and athletic games, an ice cream social, and organized family walks.

That effort comes close to capturing Levine's vision. But he would use all that extra found time for even more constructive activities: twenty-first century equivalents of barn-raisings: "If we can carve away just a third of our spectatorism and spend it, say, volunteering side-by-side with our teenagers, think what a difference we could make."

To the Miami lawyers, he said: "There is probably not a meeting room in this city with a higher concentration of talent and money, and more potential to build community. We're not asking you to carve away billable hours or family time; we're asking you to challenge your own spectatorism." When Levine said that, he reports, "a chill went through the air. But the lawyers wanted to keep talking." And they did not switch to another channel.

The Virtual Blacksmith Shop

I SPEND MUCH OF MY TIME IN A HOME OFFICE staring at a computer screen. Often on weekends, or after school, my sons head for the small Macintosh that sits a few feet away from my bigger Mac. I work in a virtual blacksmith shop.

I am not suggesting that working at home is practical or even healthy, psychologically, for everyone. But it's an option.

This was the way of fathers and children before the Industrial Revolution swept men up and sent them off to the widget factories, and later to office parks (where women later joined them). In those days, fathers—both parents— spent a lot of time close to their children. On the farm, in the store downstairs, in the blacksmith shop next door, a child might work with his father, might hand him the tools of his trade or might play to one side while his father worked. This is a different kind of traditional fatherhood than the one we usually hear about. The sinew of this earlier tradition was time and proximity. Being there. Being near.

Today, some parents take their children to the office to introduce them to the adult world of work, and to have more time with them; other parents share an avocation, in the garage shop or the kitchen, with their children. But I hear more and more parents—still more mothers than fathers—wondering aloud how they can find their way home. I'm one of the lucky post-industrial parents who gets to work at home. I should warn you: If you're thinking about working from a home office, don't assume you can get your work done and not need some additional child care, preferably in-home care.

The distractions are real. My sons are free to use the small Mac, and they're good about respecting the sanctity of my computer, but one day I couldn't figure out why the cursor on my screen was stuck. After a couple of hours of fretting and chanting Computer Voodoo, I accidentally turned my mouse over to discover that the ball inside was missing. My son and a buddy had borrowed it for a Nintendo mouse that had lost its ball. Then there are the unexpected sounds. My older son recently programmed the small computer to play, when started, the theme song to *The X-Files*. When a disk is ejected, the computer blurts out some particularly anxious dialogue from the show: "If it's not human, what is it?" When turned off, the computer says ominously, "You may not be who you are!"

There are other distractions. Scissors and tape dispensers disappear mysteriously. One time I found a neighborhood kid hiding under my desk. Our old dog, who wants to be with the boys at all times, is another issue. He licks. He sighs. He snores. He has a flatulence problem. Occasionally, this problem startles him awake and he jumps to his feet ready to flee or fight.

At times, all this happens at the same time: *The X-Files*, my boys arguing, the one-dog band, the neighborhood kids running through like herds of pygmy bison.

It's a little overwhelming.

But it's worth it. I like to think of my home office as a center of creativity and care, doorway to the world. On most days when my sons come home from school, I'm available for their homework or their skinned knees. And, most of the time, I'm fortunate to be able to attend school events or be at home when they're sick. (This is especially important because I occasionally travel for my work.)

Working from home offers immeasurable fringe benefits. The comfort of proximity and time. The Post-it™ love notes from the grade-schooler. The self-portraits stuck to my computer screen. My knowledge that they are safe. The overheard conversations between the brothers, the sudden revelations about their lives. My availability to help them with their homework and, from time to time, their projects—their comic-book catalogs, the stories they write and illustrate and print or photocopy or publish electronically, via modem, to the world.

To Matthew and Jason, the adult work world is not some mysterious and closed box, but a familiar doorway, an opportunity. They learn by osmosis as they overhear my phone interviews. They know my work personality. They understand that I sometimes feel frustrated and even defeated by work, but never permanently.

Day after day, we share our tools in our virtual blacksmith shop. Now that my older son is in junior high, I have considered moving a computer to his room. For the time being, I have decided against it. This is partly a selfish decision. Think of what I would have to give up.

Sacred Time

EVERY FAMILY NEEDS SACRED TIME. Steven Bayme believes that religious Jews and Christians should bring back the Sabbath, and that all people, religious or not, can create a kind of personal Sabbath—a family Sabbath. By that, he means a day focused entirely on the family and the spirit, when work is stopped, the TV turned off and the heart turned inward.

Bayme is director of the Jewish Communal Affairs Department of the American Jewish Committee in New York, and director of the Institute on the Jewish Family. He describes himself as a person "who strongly believes in the power of tradition."

He says a growing number of Jews are rediscovering the rituals of the Sabbath as a way, in an increasingly hectic world, to spend concentrated time with their children. For Jews, the Sabbath begins at sundown on Friday and ends at sundown on Saturday. For most Christians, the Sabbath is Sunday.

Until the late 1950s, so-called blue laws required stores to be closed on Sunday in many states. While no lobby is rushing to bring back those laws, some mainstream Christian leaders are discussing how to revive the idea of a day of rest.

One friend, a Methodist, says, "It's so easy to get caught up in the rush, even on Sunday, when I'm so busy teaching Sunday school, volunteering with a literacy program, going to district and regional church meetings, and coming into the office to put in a few hours of work. You almost need a formal ritual to break that pattern." This woman has decided that Saturday is her personal Sabbath.

Such sacred time doesn't need to be specifically religious. During the summer, my wife and I decided that we would take our kids to the beach one morning a week. We left the blankets and chairs in the car trunk. Every week, we jumped in the car and headed for the surf, and left deadlines, homework, and TV behind. Going to the beach may not be your idea of a Sabbath, but for a while it was ours.

The key was the ritual. Without that, the summer would have disappeared while we waited for a convenient time to go to the beach. "I am a father," says Bayme, "with three traditional obligations: to teach my child a living; to teach him survival skills; and to transmit Jewish tradition." To an extent, he says, the state has taken over much of the first two obligations, but not the third. This is where the Sabbath comes in.

"The act of studying Jewish text together, which is part of the Sabbath ritual, accomplishes several objectives. First, it is a statement to children that the Jewish tradition is still relevant; second, it sends out the message that the family is the setting where spiritual values are passed on from one generation to the next; third, it's a bonding experience."

Bayme quotes Abraham Joshua Heschel, a noted Jewish thinker, who called the Sabbath "sacred time," a one-day retreat from worldly pressures and influences. "In my work, I keep very late hours and travel frequently," says Bayme. "My kids will often be in bed when I get home. The amount of time we spend during the week is unfortunately quite minimal. ... But the Sabbath is a time to recharge our batteries."

He points out that Jewish tradition also describes the Sabbath as a time for sexual relations between husband and wife, also part of family life. "My children look forward to the Sabbath as a time of joy. On Friday night, we have a dinner surrounded by Jewish rituals; this is an opportunity for extended conversation, with no pressure to meet any deadlines, a time when we have friends over. We ban television on the Sabbath. We allow no external intrusions. All entertainment must be self-generated. If the weather is nice, we go out for a walk. I really look forward to this time.

"On Saturday, we go to the synagogue. There, children are treated differently than in the past; children are no longer to be seen and not heard. Now the synagogue is a place of celebration for families."

For Bayme, the Sabbath (or any ritualized, regular day of rest) must be a dramatically different texture of time than during the rest of the week. "This is a time to focus on the internal quality of our lives. This is what Heschel meant by sacred time."

To celebrate certain days, to use ritual; this is one way to value time. But rituals can grow stale. A friend tells me she's decided to forgo New Year's resolutions ("Who keeps them anyway? How many times can I resolve to go to the gym?") in favor of a journal. Beginning January 1, she intends to write one sentence a day for the rest of the year in her journal. "I'll write about one good thing that happens each day. Even on the worst days, something good happens," she says. Her husband suggested that they enter daily good things on opposite pages of the journal, but she says journals are too personal to share.

Talking to her about this, it occurred to me that there might be other ways to celebrate or mark the beginning of each new year.

Perhaps this could be the year to designate a shoe box or a drawer to hold family history photos, children's drawings, and essays, for assembly next January into a family annual. Another idea is to create a New Year's family book of records.

A few years ago, my son Jason turned a small, blue, loose-leaf binder into a Louv Book of Household Records. He has not kept it up to date, but this morning I looked through it. In 1990, he recorded that, in a matter of one year, he reduced the time it took him to get dressed from five minutes to one minute. The record that year for cleaning the house was held by JL (Jason Louv) and RL (Richard Louv) at twenty-three minutes–DNIJLR (Did Not Include Jason Louv's Room).

Jason also included in his book the record for the farthest run, held by KL (Kathy Louv), along with the records for the biggest bass, biggest trout, longest time watching television (held by ML–Matthew Louv), longest time reading, most yells, most barfs–twenty-six by JL, beating the previous record of thirteen by KL, and so on. Perhaps this year, we'll resolve to revive the *Louv Book of Household Records*.

The other day I heard a radio psychologist suggest another potential ritual: a grievance list. He recommended that family members write down things that have ticked them off during the past year, read them aloud, forgive the trespasses, then burn the lists. I'm not sure this would work well, certainly not for any family I know, particularly if the in-laws are in town. But with modification, it could make a good New Year's ceremony. Perhaps we should call them Forgiveness Lists. We could write these lists of sins–our friends', our family members', our own–and forgive them silently, then burn the lists.

This will probably be more difficult than keeping that resolution to go to the gym more often.

Forgiveness takes more practice than aerobics.

Closing Time

ONE OF THE MOST IMPORTANT LIFE CEREMONIES, a ritual for which there is no adequate name, is the act of closing a home after a loved one has died.

I remember how my brother and I went with our mother to our grandmother's old house. Because my grandmother had spent her final year in a nursing home, it had been a long time since we had been there. The air felt cold and strange as we entered the kitchen.

Over the next few days, our mother, who was usually demonstrative with her feelings, turned inward and away.

Insulated by childhood from these feelings, my brother and I helped her pack for a while, but then lost interest. We crept up the winding stairs to explore the small, secret rooms on the third floor, which we were sure were haunted.

To our great delight, we found, in the back of a closet, a stack of violent and sexually lurid detective magazines from the '30s and '40s and a Colt .45 with an old cigar can of bullets. They had belonged to our great-uncle. Deep in the house, our mother, an only child, moved from room to room, packing and discarding and remembering, alone.

I understand now how hard it must have been for her.

On a recent weekend, my brother and I took our turn. After our father and mother had died, we had delayed selling the family house for as long as economics would allow. But now came the call of escrow. It was time.

Unlike our mother, we did not have to go through this experience alone. We had each other. Such luck comes at a price. The attorney who had transferred the ownership of the house to us had looked at me from above her reading glasses and delivered a lecture I am sure she had given often. "Time after time, I see siblings fall apart over stuff." She held the word at arms length. Siblings, she said, will blame and sue and struggle and, like dogs over a bone, pull at the stuff, snap and bite and damage each other. Over stuff.

So my brother and I worked hard not to do that.

I was more eager to sell the house than he was, and we argued. But two years ago, when we first met to divide things up, we both erred on the side of generosity. "Here, you take this." "No, you should have it." I ended up with most of that batch.

Then came the final push, the closure. On the night before we were to meet at the house, he called me from northern California. I told him that there was little left there that I wanted, and that I would help him pack what he valued, but the rest could go to charity or the dump. "If I can come home with a single suitcase of stuff, that would be great," I said. "And maybe I'll even be able to leave early."

That was a mistake. To my brother, who had lived longer in the house than I, my attitude seemed uncaring. He blew up. "That's the thing about you, Rich, you always traveled light." I yelled back: "If you want this stuff, take it, Mike, but don't force it on me."

That's the way it is with the house-closing ritual. The stuff is loaded: buried in the old wood and cracked plastic is the residue of joy but also past disappointments and hurts. Neither of us, it turned out, slept well that night.

The next day, traveling light, I arrived by plane first. I walked into the house and grimaced. All that decay, boxes damaged by a leaking roof and time.

I dived into the piles, sorting and discarding, just as my mother had done decades ago. I was careful to set aside anything that my brother would value. And as I pulled and tossed and sweated, I realized that I valued some of the remains more than I had thought I would. That did not mean I wanted them, but I knew my brother would and I was relieved. I worked fast; I decided my part of the deal would be to save my brother some of the pain of sorting.

Later in the day, he drove up in his battered pickup. He was relieved to see the organized piles ready for him to review. We did this together, taking renewed care with one another's feelings. I found a folder of records that straightened out an old dispute between us about a college trust fund; neither of us had been at fault. This is one of the good things about the ritual: mysteries are sometimes solved, the answers found on crumbling paper.

We piled the throwaway stuff into his truck and tied it down with rope and old extension cords. We stood back and looked at the leaning tower of stuff. I joked that we should sing the theme song to *The Beverly Hillbillies*.

He laughed. It was a good sight, and not painful. It was good to send it on its way.

Later, we filled the truck again with what we both valued, now cleaned and boxed. After we drove away, I realized that I had not looked back.

At the airport, we hugged each other and he insisted on helping me with our father's suitcase, filled with the old photographs and paintings by our mother.

"You don't have to help me," I said.

"It looks heavy," he said, and he carried it. Then he was gone, but as I was searching for my flight number on the departures screen, he loped back into the airport. "Rich, let's go fishing soon." I grinned and nodded. He grinned, too. We had survived the necessary passage.

I am fascinated by heirlooms. Why do we take some things with us into the future, and not others? Some things are kept because they are worth money, or at least that is why we think we keep them. But most heirlooms carry within them a family's mythic DNA, the evolution of its story.

In my parents' house, I could find very little of my father's. He kept no family photos. He told us little of his heritage. My brother and I grew up holding our breath, hiding the knives, finding guns in the attic, and removing them, or coming home to the smell of gas. After decades of this, our father finally succeeded in ending his own life, but even then we did not exhale.

I did find a plate of his: a square platter, trimmed in gold. He had kept this plate on his night stand for as long as I could remember. Each night, he removed his watch and put it there, and his pens, and his change.

For years I have tried to push his illness away from me. Talking to a friend, I said, "My mother and brother and I were all so angry at him. I'm surprised that I put the plate on my night stand, so close to my head when I sleep. And, now, each night I remove my watch and put it there, and my pens, and my change." My friend looked at me as if I had missed the obvious. "It is the thing that represents the times when your father was dependable." I suddenly knew that she was right. Surely, beneath the cloud of my father's illness was a small island of dependability.

Each night when I place my watch on that plate, I touch that land, and each morning when I reach for it, I scoop up a handful of island soil, and take it with me into the future.

Seeing Time

WITH PATIENCE, PERSEVERANCE AND REVERENCE, you can see time. You can *almost* stop it.

Somewhere in the twilight, as we headed across the Nevada's Mojave desert, Gary Adams' eyes noted the pattern of the creosote bushes. Adams sees things like this; he sees what you and I so often do not see, patterns from afar, details and rhythms and zones of gray.

Director of cardiac rehabilitation at Las Vegas' University Medical Center, and a photographer by avocation, he studied with the late Ansel Adams, premier photographer of the West. Gary Adams was not related directly to Ansel Adams, but, like the creosote that we pass a few miles down the road, he was of the same species, and his career grew in a similar pattern.

In the gathering darkness as we drove through the desert, he told of growing up in Los Angeles, watching the eucalyptus trees and the orange groves disappear. "Everything there from my childhood is gone."

His life was shaped by one moment, thirty-four years ago. "I was on a photography field trip. I was riding in the back of a pickup truck, with wooden slats all around, sleeping through the night, awakening in the Owens Valley as the temperature dropped."

What he saw was the Sierra and Mount Whitney in the dawn. Most other kids would have rolled over and gone back to sleep, but ten-year-old Gary Adams sat up, transfixed by that shining thing against the silver sky.

Today, his ambition is to continue in the Ansel Adams tradition. He likes to paraphrase Mary Austin, a chronicler of the Southwest: "I want to know large tracts of land as intimately as a New Yorker would know a city park."

We approached the Utah border, passing through Mesquite, Nevada, population 1,200. Up against the highway pushed a massive, glittering casino sign the size of a three-story building: Peppermill Resort Hotel and Casino super low rates 344 deluxe rooms diesel fuel 67.5 children free.

The light blinked in Gary Adams' glasses as we passed, and then his glasses turned black with the desert.

That night we stayed at his small cabin in the village of Springdale, at the canyon mouth of Zion National Park. At dawn, through the window, came the first sight: scarlet fingers and fists of sandstone ramming into the clouds.

Adams drove the Honda down the valley of the Virgin River. He parked near a long meadow, got out of the car and walked across the expanse. He stood there in a field of purple filaree and looked at the peaks through a Wratten 90 filter, which he wears on a cord around his neck. Looking through this square of amber glass, Adams could see tones visible only to a camera's lens.

He turned abruptly and walked back to the Honda. Working silently, he unpacked sixty pounds of wooden and metal boxes of camera gear, and a heavy surveyor's tripod, and headed back the quarter mile. Setting up for a shot is a laborious, lengthy process. Often, the shot does not work.

"The light I like the best is in the winter when the sun is in the South, when a very soft light comes across the desert." He lugged the gear across the filaree, knees bent, chugging. "In the spring, the wind can be a problem."

"At first, the wind is impressive, you hear it building at night. You have this hopefulness that when you awake it will be stopped but it doesn't stop. It batters you down. You can't open a car door, you can't photograph in it, you set up a large-frame camera and it's like setting up sail."

But on this day, the wind was in the peaks, sweeping the clouds across, changing the light. In the field, the air was calm.

Adams opened the tripod, stabbed its prongs into the filaree, and set up his Deardorf, an 8x20-inch view camera, handmade for Kodak in the 1950s of Nicaraguan mahogany—aged half a century before being used. Today such a camera, custom made, could cost $8,000 before adding a lens.

Adams, who died of cancer a few years after our trip, was one of a handful of serious landscape photographers in the West still using large-format (larger than 11x14 inches) view cameras. The larger the negative, the more precise the detail. Over the years, photographs produced by large-format cameras and shown before Congress have helped save much of the West. Sometimes a picture is worth a thousand filibusters.

He carefully unwrapped a 475-millimeter, fifty-five-year-old Goerz Dagor lens, whisked it with a camel hair brush, and screwed it onto the front of the Deardorf. He uncovered the lens and pulled out the bellows, and then turned his attention to the scene.

Here is an approximation of what he saw: The stunning Towers of the Virgin and the West Temple, a grand cathedral of twisted spires, crowned with a halo of moisture. The great cliffs were streaked with "desert varnish," black stains made of dead lichen and micro-organisms.

From instant to instant, the light would change, radically. A long wedge of cottonwoods in the valley would alternatively burst into a glow of creamy light and then fade into dullness. Adams was watching the cottonwoods, not the peaks. He disappeared beneath a "dark cloth," draped over the camera, and studied this scene, the image upside down on the ground glass.

Moving quickly now, he pointed a hand-held light meter at the cottonwood and took a reading. He slid a large film holder, which held a sheet of Super XX film (specially cut by Kodak) into the camera. He pulled out the "dark slide," which exposed the film to the void in the camera.

Finger on the shutter release, ready, ready.

Suddenly the sun moved behind a cloud. The cottonwoods shuddered in the wind, the peaks darkened, and the scene was destroyed.

At a time like this, most rational people would consider punt-kicking the camera straight into the Virgin River, but Adams moved away from the tripod, stood there with the light meter to his eye, waiting.

Sometimes he waits for hours. Sometimes he waits for years, coming back to a spot time after time, waiting for that precise moment, hoping that the off-road vehicles and the highways and the condos don't get there first.

The clouds parted. His hand moved toward the Deardorf, almost in slow motion, and he opened the lens a half second at f-45. Click and another click. And he captured the photograph.

"This is heaven," he said. "Heaven."

It was a moment.

The Strand
of Spirit

We are each of us angels with only one wing, and we can only
fly embracing each other.

—Luciano De Crescenzo

The Angel

ONE EVENING, I WENT INTO MATTHEW'S ROOM to tuck him into bed. It is a startling room, green and pink and yellow, colors that he picked, which fit his iridescent nature. In the dim light, the colors now were muted and I saw the glint of his thick, round glasses. He was seven years old at the time, and like many children that age, he could see some things better than his parents.

"Can I take your glasses off so your nose can grow?" I asked. I say this nearly every night, just before I remove them and fold them and put them in the corner of his bed frame, where he can find them easily in the morning. This is one of our comforting rituals.

"Dad, I want to tell you something." Sleep was already on its way. His voice was a little blurry, but serious, matter-of-fact. "Last night, I met my guardian angel," he said.

"You did?" I smiled, then reminded myself not to discount or deflect. "Can you tell me about it?"

"Yes. Last night I was scared. So I came and got in bed between you and Mom." Lately, he has been fighting midnight monsters, the ones that small children must slay or outlast, the ones that sometimes return in midlife.

He sighed and pulled his blanket up closer to his chin. "I went to sleep and then I woke up and that's when I saw my guardian angel."

I thought about this. "Was it male or female?"

"I don't know. It was sitting at the end of the bed. It was long and light colored. It was looking out the window and smiling. And then it was gone."

We had not been talking about angels. I don't know that we had ever talked about them. Perhaps he absorbed the image from the current culture.

Angels are a growth industry. Malls overflow with angel books, angel calendars and dolls and napkin rings and thank-you notes. Saks Fifth Avenue sells "Angel" perfume from a French clothing designer who believes everyone has a guardian angel or "at least can smell like one."

Polls show that more than half of Americans believe in angels.

Regarding angels, I am agnostic. But I do believe my son.

I know that this thing at the foot of our bed has been there for a long time. Winged figures appear in the tombs of Egyptians and Assyrians and Sumerians. Jews, Christians and Muslims have pondered the nature of angels, as have Buddhists and Hindus. Generations of Catholic children have learned the "Prayer to the Guardian Angel," and some have been advised to keep a space open in their school desks for their angels.

Some theologians exhort the current fascination with angels as a sign of Western culture's spiritual reawakening. Others dismiss it as New Age cultism, the trivialization of God. Some critics are uncomfortable with the idea of preferential treatment. Why would one child enjoy the protection of an angel, when another child, perhaps one living near the heart of darkness, have none?

As if it can be resolved, the debate will continue long after the current fad has faded. And children will still believe in guardian angels.

Sitting next to my son, I recalled my own childhood. Unlike Matthew, I never met my guardian angel; I only believed in it.

Perhaps Matthew is passing through an identifiable stage of child development. If I cared to look, I might find a parenting book that would explain, all on the same page, guardian angels, imaginary friends, and pets that talk. Perhaps, I would be assured, this is all very predictable; children need to psychologically create these helpers as they encounter the looming adult world, the growing sense of separateness, the dark and waiting shapes in the closet.

But I do not want to read that page. Like many parents, I may profess skepticism that adults are protected by angels, but I want desperately to believe that my children are special, that someone—some gentle and comforting spirit—is helping watch over them.

"How did you know it was your guardian angel?" I asked. I took off Matthew's glasses and folded them and placed them in their safe place.

"I just knew, and ever since then, I have believed in heaven."

He rolled over. His breathing came easy as he floated to sleep. No midnight monsters tonight.

Parents cannot parent, at least not well, alone. They cannot do it well without other parents, without community, or without a spiritual connection. Personally, it doesn't matter much to me if God is a man or a woman or a politically correct cross-dresser. But I do recognize, as a father, that there is something within me or without me, something that does, upon occasion, guide my parenting.

A rabbi I know says, "I'm raising my children with the hope, not that they'll emulate me as a man or my wife as a woman, but that they're involved in a religious community." He speaks of the bar mitzvah and bat mitzvah ceremonies (which mean: "son of" or "daughter of" the community). Why, I wonder, during a conversation about spirituality, does the word community come up so soon? Because, explains a Jesuit priest, the home has become more of a 'small h' home." As a culture we focus too much on the isolated family, the individual parent, and not enough on what he calls the "Home with a capital H." The neighborhood, the world, the universe. The priest describes how, in his studies of Native American cultures, he learned how fathers took their sons out to the world, to the woods, to introduce them to the "house beyond the teepee."

Listening to him, I remember an experience with my first-born, when he was ten. We were taking a family drive in the mountains and stopped at a desert viewpoint. My wife and younger son stayed behind and I took Jason down a path, to a place I knew about. We walked to the very edge of the cliff—or, rather, I led him to the edge. I held his arm as we sat down; then I let his arm go. We dangled our feet over the edge. We could see, far below, two ravens picking their way up a ravine. We watched shadows move out over the desert. I could feel his tension ease.

One man tells me the only miracle he had ever experienced were the births of his children. But it seems to me that childbirth is only the first of the miracles. Each growth spurt, each burst of consciousness in my sons, is also a miracle. Even my older son's early adolescence, his tentative pulling away, is a miracle of one more birth. Something more fully formed is emerging from the cocoon, with unfolding antennae and wet and crumpled wings, reaching back to me but emerging, emerging.... Is this any less a miracle than that one, so many short years ago, when I first saw the slick crown of his head?

The Music of Inner Life

MAYBE SOMETHING IS IN THE AIR other than hydrocarbons and rap. I keep running into people who, in many ways, are asking this question: In a culture overwhelmed by a wall of media sound and fury, where children grow up believing that free speech is wearing a T-shirt festooned with a favorite commercial slogan—how does a person nurture an interior life?

No people is as keenly aware of this problem as the continent's native people, who for centuries have fought, with varying success, to retain their identities, culturally and individually. "I come from a culture that is personally defined," said R. Carlos Nakai, of Navajo-Ute descent. He was wearing jeans and a formal wing-collar shirt. His hair was braided. We were sitting in the Phoenix, Arizona, office of Canyon Records, which markets Nakai as the premier Native American flutist and composer—a crossover artist fusing the cedar flute, made of wood 300 or 400 years old, with a New Age sound. Not since Buffy Saint Marie, in the 1960s, has a Native American gained such a following in the majority culture. But don't call him a New Age artist and don't call him a Native American.

"The culture of my people was here before America was invented. I refer to myself as Diné, which means human being or people. Native Americans are people of European descent who came to this country after 1600. I am an indigenous person, a native. The most correct term to refer to people of my culture is by their tribal name." But mainly, Nakai is Nakai.

"I work in personal music, a mixture of my experiences in the outer world and the inner world." The Navajos, as Nakai points out, are masters of assimilation. Before Columbus came to America, the Diné left the northern Athabascan tribes of Alaska and western Canada and migrated southward, mingling with and absorbing the cultures of the Pueblo peoples.

"I come from a culture that is personally defined, with no dogma or cultural doctrine. No one native person anywhere in the world can speak for the whole culture. Each native person is responsible for developing a personalized state of awareness. In a culture where very little is private, where everything belongs to everyone, that's all we have. Your mind is your own."

"In the American society, you live in an externalized world, an outer world, according to a set of rules and guidelines. You're continually comparing yourself to other people and to the doctrine and the dogma of your society."

Nakai refers to himself as a member of "an inner culture." Yet what he describes isn't what most of us regard as individualism. Paradoxically, Nakai's personalized inner life—his individualism—is intimately connected to his sense of tribal tradition—an evolving tradition.

"I come from a long line of singers," he explained. "In my tribal group, the singer is most important because he carries the history and the various philosophies of how to survive. We tell people these old stories; the people take them and personalize them. I'm doing these ceremonies now with the American people. I'm helping to bring them into the indigenous culture of this country, because they are hungry to feel a part of the land they are in."

The stories he tells in his music are stories of nature—the subsonic vibrations he has felt on the expanses of the northern plains and the Southwest, the "blood memory of the sound of wolves," and the elemental nature that exists even in the brick and plastic of cities.

It's time, he suggests, for both American and native cultures to pick up the past and move into the future—to evolve as nature does. "What happened in 1786 on the plains or in 1820 down in Canyon de Chelly—that's irrelevant now. Who cares? You base your life only on the past, you're not going anywhere. You're always worrying about measuring up."

Likewise, he says, "in this country we listen to European music from the past while there are American composers today that we should be listening to, because that's the music of this country. Jazz is the truest American music form—improvisational, nomadic, it moves freely from one culture group to the next. It speaks with the American language—a mixture of all the languages on the planet, including the language of the indigenous people, which is used to explain geographic features and philosophy."

This moving on will depend on people like Nakai, who reject what passes now for individualism.

Listening to Nakai, I thought of something I had read a few hours earlier. Lawrence Christon of the *Los Angeles Times* had described the audience's response at an Andrew Dice Clay performance, the howl of a generation— young men and women "malled in, cineplexed, media-manipulated, undereducated, self-disgusted and cut off from the wellspring of an inner life."

Oddly, Nakai meets some of the same kind of criticism leveled at Clay. "In much of the indigenous community, I'm an outsider. I'm regarded as one who is taking the culture and destroying it. The criticism that is leveled is that I am conversing with people who should be regarded as enemies. The real threat is that I am breaking down the walls between cultures."

He has, in fact, been witched by some Navajos. Though he does not give these acts any credence, his parents worry about him. Within the confines of isolated Navajo culture, sorcery carries great psychological power.

"At a concert in Europe, a man came up and blew something all over me." The man, who was German, said, 'I got you now.'"

"Sure did," said Nakai. "Was that your food?"

"I put a spell on you. Aren't you afraid?"

"No," Nakai answered. "That only works in a closed society."

"Then you're not a real Indian!" said the German.

But Nakai did not mind. He moved on.

When he visits schools around the country, he asks children what every Navajo asks another Navajo when meeting for the first time: "Who are you?"

And the kids answer, "I don't know."

"They're taught history, but no one talks to them about how to define themselves in this world. I tell them: Each of you is the creator of your own world, and each of you is the one who will carry your world into the future."

He plays his music to them, and sometimes the children sit spellbound and silent even after he has left the stage.

"They are listening to themselves."

We drop like pebbles into the ponds of each other's souls, and the orbit of our ripples continues to expand, intersecting with countless others.

—Joan Borysenko

A Place Afire

THE FIREKEEPER, A YOUNG NAVAJO wearing rubber boots, stoked a fire of pine and cedar and alder wood. The men had gone into the lodge, and only two of us remained, waiting to go in. All of us had stripped completely, and it was cold standing out on the field of clover and mud, the Northwest wind moving through. The guard tower and the guns above. The fence with rolls of razor wire surrounding the place. And in the distance, mountains capped with snow, some of them forested, some clear-cut.

I was standing in the yard of the Twin Rivers Corrections Center near Monroe, Washington, looking at a sweat lodge—a place of purification. The size of a large pup tent, the lodge was made of willow boughs, covered with tarpaulins and blankets. One of the preparers pointed to a collection of plastic water buckets filled with ice-cold water. "Pour that over your head and body," said one of the men. "You'll be glad you did, later. And take a towel. Here, put it in the water. You'll need it. When the heat gets to be too much, hold it up to your mouth and nose. That way you won't pass out."

Another man, the doorkeeper, led me around the lodge—clockwise, the direction the earth moves around the sun. He told me to take a pinch of tobacco from a pouch hung on a pole, and to sprinkle it on an altar of rocks, pine poles, and deer antlers: the spirit house.

I moved past two half-moon shaped mounds of dirt—

representing the physical life and the unseen life—and entered the open flap of the lodge on hands and knees. "This way." Hands guided me to the back of the little lodge, to sit next to the cedar man, the medicine man's assistant.

In the dim, smokey light, twelve Native Americans, "skins" as the members of this group call themselves, sat cross-legged in a circle, hunched over in the mud. Bob Shimek, the Anishinabe (or Chippewa) medicine man, the first Native American medicine man in the United States to be hired by a prison system, sat next to the door. As he explained later, the sweat lodge, with the pit and the rocks glowing within it, is the womb of Mother Earth; the rocks are the seed of life, the water is fertilizer, and from that combination comes birth and renewal.

Now the fire watcher began to carry rocks in from the fire. Shimek employed deer antlers, like two forks, to transfer the rocks to the pit. They were round lava rocks—brought here from nearby Mount Rainier. The cedar man tossed a pinch of cedar across each new rock.

I looked around at the men. There were murderers here, and men of other sins. A man named Modoc sat to my right, shaped like a bear, with the hands of an artist, his throat scarred from ear to ear, his wrists encircled with tattooed bricks and chains. Earlier, he had said that the medicine man had given him back his Achumawi soul. The temperature began to rise. The men steamed sweat, their eyes were half-lidded. The flap was dropped.

Only the dimly glowing rocks could be seen; among them, a small rack of deer antlers seemed to expand and contract. (Later, Shimek told me that there were no deer antlers in the rocks; my wife commented that this symbolized my need for my glasses.) A drum began to pound. The cedar man began his prayer. Now suddenly a galaxy of stars spread—exploded—across the center of world. The air was filled with the dizzying scent of a secret combination of herbs—tobacco and lavender and something Shimek calls sweat-lodge medicine. Water hit the rocks and the air hit the lungs and stung the skin; hair felt afire.

Led by Shimek, the Diné, the Lakota and the Suquamish began to sing an Anishinabe song. The song swelled with the drum, upper notes almost falsetto, harmonic bass lines moving from the left; the song seemed sad and full and there were sharp cries within it as it grew louder and fuller, and it could have been 10,000 years ago, or a century ago or a century to come, and then the song ended and the men, in the dark, spoke their approval: 'Ho!" "Ah-ho!" "Ho-ahh!"

The drum moved left. A voice said: "Tunkasila, thank you for this visitor; help him write the truth and not hurt us; and thank you for Bob Shimek, who comes to us with a twinkle of hope in his eyes." The drum thumped and he said: "All my relations."

This was the signal for the drum to be passed. More prayers were said to the Great Spirit, for strength, for families, for the creatures of the world. The air scalded the throat, turning it inside out. Now Modoc's voice, almost childlike, croaked, as if from a long way off, praying to "Grandfather" for homeless children, and to "help our brothers who find themselves caught up in circumstances they cannot understand." "Ho!" "Ho-ahh!" The cedar man's eagle-bone whistle called the spirits; ears split, the air split and for this moment, at least, the men, all of us, were purified.

At times during these ceremonies evil things reveal themselves, Shimek told me later, things that he can see— which sometimes leap from one man into another man's body or assume physical shape, as roots, rocks, snakes— and Shimek takes them into himself, and then secretly exorcises them.

The drum came to me, and somehow I pounded a stupid TOM-tom-tom-tom-TOM-tom-tom-tom beat from boyhood. Perhaps it was only what I heard, and they did not hear it. I slowed down, beat evenly. More water hit the rocks and the air cracked: I expressed gratitude for my wife and children and asked to be able to write about this experience without romanticizing it. *"Ho! Ahh-ho!"* came voices of sudden approval. "All my relations." The prayers and the cries and the drumming and the flashes of sudden light continued, on and on. The songs seemed to slip beneath the air and lift it up above our heads.

Finally—an hour, a year later?—the flap opened and the legs of the firekeeper appeared. Shimek dipped a fir bough into ice-cold water and sprayed us for a final purification. The singing continued for a while, then almost in slow motion some of the men, on their hands and knees, crawled out the door.

A few of them collapsed face-down in pools of water and clover beneath the gun towers. The razor wire glistened with water and sun. The sky was brighter now. I moved out into the cold air and sat on a bench with my head down for a while, the earth moving. Singing and the faint thump, thump, thump of a drum still drifted across the field from the lodge.

"What do you think?" one of the men asked, sitting at the other end of the bench, skin scalded red as a lobster, his face buried in a towel.

"Beats church," I wanted to say. Instead, I said, "It's fine."

"Only time in my life I feel free," the prisoner said, head still buried in the towel, looking up now. "I'm not even here."

Several weeks later a package came in the mail that contained one of Modoc's exquisite woodcuts; this one of a shaman. Below the image he had written this: "The Warrior's Shield is his fearlessness to accept responsibility and challenge even the unknown. Spiritualism is wealth and power.... The true measure of strength is pride in being who, what, and how you are.... Sacredness is solely given to those who suffer for others in this threshold of eternity.... Freedom is knowing that with every step you are one breath closer to reaching that ultimate goal.

The Belt

FOR FOUR DECADES, JACKSON CLARK, a fourth-generation Durangoan, has been a trader of Navajo rugs and jewelry. He is sixty-nine and suffers from prostate cancer. His disease is static, but he moves more slowly now, and his focus has shifted from rugs and jewelry to fragile stories more likely than stone to disappear in the dust storms or the dancing rain.

He has written a little book, *The Owl in Monument Canyon* (University of Utah Press), about the skinwalkers and traders, weavers and medicine men, priests and adventurers and friends he has known. In the introduction to Clark's book, writer and naturalist Terry Tempest Williams writes that Clark's stories "create a bridge between cultures. A healing."

Now Jackson Clark's Saab was bumping down a dirt road into the Santo Domingo Pueblo, south of Santa Fe.

This is where, years ago, he would visit Santiago Moguino, a Pueblo Indian who first came into Jackson Hardware (which his father owned and where Clark first learned to trade) on a cold winter night in 1946, wrapped in a well-worn Pendleton blanket with his long hair tied in a knot. "You wanna trade, Jack?"

"The name is Jackson, not Jack."

For years they haggled. Clark remembers how they squatted on the floor with a pile of rugs and jewelry. "I spotted an extraordinary turquoise necklace and reached to put it in my pile. 'No! Put it back!' Santiago said. He reached across the rugs and slapped my hand. When he reached for a rug, I did the same thing to him. We had a royal hand-slapping contest. We laughed and swore and tried to be angry with each other, but it was simply too much fun."

Clark was especially attracted to a heavy, ornate belt that the old man always wore. Everything except the belt was negotiable.

Twenty years later, Moguino came to Clark and said, "Jack, I need money to fix my tractor. You lend me $600 and I leave my belt with you. If anything happens to me, you keep the belt. Don't give it to my boys. They will just sell it." Clark put the belt in his safe. Not long afterward, Moguino died and the belt remains there today.

"Once or twice a year, for special occasions, I take it out, polish it and wear it. Someone almost always tries to buy it." The belt is not negotiable. Santo Domingo Pueblo has changed in only small ways since Clark first began to visit Moguino there. Santo Domingo, he says, continues to be the most conservative and secretive of all the pueblos. Ladders emerge from the ceremonial kivas; 300-year-old homes are held together by occasional mud plasters; little yards are contained by coyote fences of oak or cedar poles.

Clark stopped to visit with Joseph Coriz, a jewelry maker and silversmith who carries on Moguino's tradition.

"Woo-eee! Haven't seen you for a long time, Jackson!" said Coriz.

His two children ran in and out of his front room, speaking the pueblo language, Keres. On the walls of the room were the heads of two deer, Coriz's beautiful necklaces hanging from their necks.

Coriz rolled up his sleeves and showed Clark the deep, red scars on his arms from a recent automobile accident. Clark told him briefly about his own health problems. Coriz showed Clark his latest bolo ties, with clasps depicting the turtles on which his people entered the universe, and Clark, perhaps out of habit, made an offer, and they settled on a price.

"I have been doing turtles lately. People like turtles," he said. His silver turtles carry corn and pueblo houses on their backs. "Some things I am not allowed to do—bears, eagles, cougar," he said to me. I asked why. "I can't really tell you why," he said. "It is against my religion."

He said he is often offered huge sums of money by rich tourists from Santa Fe. But some things are not negotiable.

As we drove out of the pueblo, Clark said, "Sometimes when I am here, I look for Santiago Moguino in the crowd. Sometimes I think I see him." Clark said he wanted to take me to one of his favorite places. We passed through tortured badlands along a road lined with crosses. During Holy Week, this road is lined with people, mainly Hispanic country people, who walk as far as 200 miles to the little church, Santuario de Chimyo. The church has stood here for nearly two centuries.

We parked and went into the church. We sat quietly in the coolness, and looked at the crude and ancient frescoes, these images of man's startling realization of his own suffering.

After a while, Clark took me into the back room of the church and showed me a small pit of dust. The pilgrims come here because, like the Tewa Indians who preceded the Spanish, they believe it will heal them. I remembered how his friend Mary Begay had whispered her story about the skinwalkers and how the medicine man had made a sand painting on the floor of her hogan, and how when she had healed had scattered the sand.

"They eat this dust or rub it on their bodies," said Clark, standing in the back room of Santuario de Chimyo. He reached down and picked up some of the dirt, and he rubbed it quickly, almost furtively, on his groin, where his cancer resides, and he smiled.

Although the world is full of suffering, it is also very full of the overcoming of it.

–Helen Keller

The Process of Life

WE LIVE IN A TIME IN WHICH THE PROCESS of life seems less important than the products that life produces. So it's important to be reminded now and again of the process. One day, I received a letter from a woman who wished to share a story of her daughter's achievement, the kind for which there are no diplomas.

"Five years ago," Diana Jeansonne wrote, "Susanna's petite little cheerleading life was shattered" when she was struck by a car. At that time, Susanna, who was then 12, was living with her family in Glendale, Arizona. Jeansonne accompanied her letter with a clipping from *The Arizona Republic* from December 19, 1990, headlined "The Comeback Kid." The writer, Linda Helser, had gotten to know her family. As she told the story, a paramedic who responded to the accident felt helpless because all he could see of the little girl, pinned beneath the car, was "her arms up against the exhaust pipe and it was burning her arms." For two months, Susanna remained in a coma.

"I wanted to stay in the coma because I didn't want to know what was going on," she told Helser. "There was this bright light and this man asked me if I wanted to stay here or go back to Earth. I told him I wanted to go back because I missed my mom and my dog."

During brain surgery, she nearly bled to death. Twice, surgeons believed that she was brain-dead. She "flat-lined" three times. Her body swelled to the point where the only body part that her mother could recognize was her hand, with worn-off purple nail polish. Her father, a senior pastor at a church in Glendale, had doubts about how long Susanna could hold onto life. "He held up pretty good," Diana recalled, "until the doctor told us that they had removed the bone from the right side of her head because of brain swelling, and they'd freeze it and replace it if she lived. He just lost it, because he felt like they were taking his daughter away, piece by piece."

Yet there was a glue within Susanna, an adhesive to life, a process. On January 8, Diana watched her daughter's pale blue eyes open. Over the next many months in intensive care, through multiple brain and lung surgeries, the hospital staff called her "The Miracle Brat." Her family smuggled her dog, Sammy, into the hospital; the nurses covered for her. She decided to run for student-body secretary from her hospital bed. A friend read her campaign speech for her, and she won. Eight months later, she left the hospital in a wheelchair. She took $250 from the $2,400 that had been raised for her by a motorcycle club and bought fifty T-shirts for the hospital staff. The shirts read: "We Save Lives, St. Joe's, Pediatric ICU—Thanks, Susanna, one more satisfied customer." But despite what her doctors said, she refused to think of her recovery, which was still in process, as a miracle. Over the next few years, she endured other surgeries and treatments, the removal of deep scars on her arms, the straightening of her left leg. She used an oxygen machine when sleeping. She struggled.

Recently, she graduated from high school. In anticipation of the ceremony, her mother wrote to me: "On graduation night, few in attendance will fully understand what a milestone her graduation will be. On her special night, I can't help but grieve because there won't be a scholarship for strength of character. No award will be given for courage, and no plaque in recognition of a spunky recovering spirit. These values and traits are grossly overlooked, and yet my daughter and other special needs 'survivor' kids exude them every day."

Susanna would probably not want a plaque, and her mother understands that. "She won't get academic or athletic awards this month," Diana wrote, "and her scars will forever prevent beauty pageants, but she has learned what really matters in life. Family, friendship, strength of character, courage and spunk. They are hers and the realization causes me to privately smile."

A few weeks ago, Susanna sent a letter to all of those who had been part of her care and recovery. Excitedly, she wrote that she been accepted to her first-choice college, Linfield College in Oregon, "where they have a special program and a special woman on staff with a doctorate in helping college-bound kids with learning deficits. . . . I'm especially excited to live in beautiful, rainy Oregon. Most people think I'm nuts." And she added, "There just aren't enough thank yous that can be said for all your intense prayers on my behalf. Please know that when I reach my hand out to grab my diploma and then move my tassel to the other side, I will be thinking of you."

Ultimately, Susanna's message is that she is not a

product; she is a living process. Her mother sent me this poem, which Susanna wrote when she was 13:

I am a human body. I heal.
I suffer trauma. I live.
Machines breath for me. I heal.
My heart stops . . .
and starts. I live.
I get infected. I fight.
My brain swells. I heal.
My mind shuts down. I fight.
My eyes open. I heal.
My muscles wither away. I heal.
Slowly they come back.
I fight.
Painful movement, inch by inch. . . .
 I fight, I heal, I live.

Bless This House

ON THE MORNING OF SEPTEMBER 19, Father Henry Rodriguez walked out of the offices of the San Diego Organizing Project, at the corner of 29th and Imperial, where police were examining the bloodstained sidewalk.

He looked into the bright sun and saw a woman coming toward him, pulling two small children behind her. Her face was filled with fear and fatigue and she asked him to perform a blessing on her house, to help protect her family por favor, Padre, por favor, Padre....

He explained that he had to be somewhere soon, but that he could give her and the two children a quick blessing. The house itself could wait.

So now, two weeks later, Father Henry and I sat with Consuela (whose name I have changed) at her table. Her home was threadbare but neat. The walls were decorated with religious icons and her children's educational certificates, including one from Head Start. One of her older boys was asleep on the couch.

She is forty-three. Her eyes are kind and intelligent.

During the past two years, she said (with Father Henry translating), she and her children have witnessed at least ten acts of violence, including four murders—drug murders, drive-by shootings with automatic weapons. Through the days and evenings, she watches the young men from her window, sees how casually they draw handguns from inside their sleeves or pant legs.

Does she ever talk to the young men, ever confront them?

No, she said. She touched the base of her throat.

As she talked, her oldest son, shirtless, stood up from the couch and moved to the front door. He stepped out on the porch, hands hanging beside his hips. He looked up the street, down the street.

The fear is palpable in this neighborhood, as if a score of serial killers have been loose here for a long, long time.

Father Henry says his church gets calls at least every other day from fearful parishioners asking for house blessings. The frequency is increasing.

And why not? On those occasions when Consuela called the police, nothing improved. The young men would run into the alleys or their apartments, or they would pretend that they were just walking along the sidewalks. The drug dealers who did get arrested were usually back on the corner before the police returned. So Consuela quit calling the police.

When the shooting happened on September 18, it was like a movie, she said—very grim, very sad. She and some visitors were sitting there talking, having a good time. It was around eight o'clock. Her kids were outside. She heard the fast gunfire, the wap—wap—wap.

She ran out to pull her kids into the house. She saw two bodies, young black men, one lying still on the corner sidewalk, the other one across the street. She ran to one of the men to see if he was still alive.

He was shot right here, she said, placing her hand

on her sternum. He was twenty or twenty-one, wearing a blue shirt. Someone rolled him over and she saw a hole near where the bullet had exited. She placed her fingers on the back of her shoulder. Right there. He was still breathing, and she said this filled her with even more fear, because she didn't know what to do to help him or if he could still hurt her.

Her children ran up to see the bodies. She shooed them back in. She went back inside her house. She couldn't sit down. She was trembling. The police came. The wounded man was taken away. She doesn't know if he survived. (He did not.) Someone covered the other body with a sheet and the police marked the sidewalk around the body with yellow tape.

Then the crowd came, and circled around the police and the yellow tape and the body. Some of them were carrying baseball bats and other weapons. The crowd, fifty or so adults and youths, were screaming: Mexicans you've done this. Mexicans we'll kill you.

Hearing that, she drew away from the windows and the door. She felt cold. Then someone knocked on the door. It was her neighbor, her best friend, a black woman who said: Don't worry. I'll protect you.

The body was left on the sidewalk until around 3 A.M. For the rest of that night, she and her children didn't sleep. Her youngest boy cried on and off, saying: Mama, they're going to come get us, too.

All night she asked herself: How can I live in the midst of this? Why do these people kill each other so easily?

When dawn came, she began to feel a little better. She parted the curtains. The blood was still there. The street was empty. She saw the priest standing on the corner. She thought he had come to bless the place where the young men had been shot. She grabbed a child's hand, and ran to the door....

Now, sitting with Father Henry, Consuela told him that her own sons are not involved in drugs or gangs. They're in school. They get good grades. But when she recently asked her oldest son to get a job, he answered: Why should I do that, when I can make so much more selling drugs?

She wants her children to have a new life. But moving will be difficult. She and her children live on a welfare check of $1,000 a month. But she has a friend with a rental apartment two or three miles away. Maybe her friend will rent it to her cheap. That neighborhood looks more peaceful, but she isn't sure.

In the meantime, Consuela does what she can. Near the window, she has placed plaster figures of Jesus and Mary. On the mantle next to an old photograph of her mother she burns a devotional candle.

She left the room for a moment. Her son was out on the porch again, watching the street. She returned with a generic-brand mayonnaise jar. This, she explained, was holy water. Just a small amount, but good holy water.

Father Henry took the mayonnaise jar from her hands and opened it. Praying in Spanish, he walked from room to room flipping water with his fingers.

Then the two of them stood for a moment, side by

side. She looked down, eyes closed; he looked at the ceiling and prayed, blessing her house and the woman and the children who live within it, in the name of the Father and the Son and the Holy Spirit. . . .

Amen.

A few miles away, a statue of Jesus stands in front of a church. Long ago, someone painted the face black. Then, in the 1960s, someone cut off the hands and stole them. Later, someone propped a crude sign at the base of the statue. The sign is still there. It says: "I have no hands but yours."

The Navajos call dawn "grandfather talking god." When the strip of white light rises over the mountains, there is no evil, no pain; the dust of the previous day has settled.

May the Spirit Move You, One Way or Another

THE THIN CRESCENT SLICE OF MOON seemed a rip in the blackness; deep maroon spread above the island; the mirrored surface of the lake seemed lit from below. The air was cool; trout began to rise. Coyotes howled and then stopped as suddenly as they had begun. I reached up and banged on the underside of the van's pop-up bunk.

"Boys, wake up. Look outside." But of course they did not stir. My older son's hand hung over the edge of the bunk, fingers twitching in sleep. I smiled at his hand, and continued to watch the morning grow and expand.

In truth, a sunrise is a mundane occurrence. Happens every day. Sometimes the sunrise is hidden by clouds or smog or sleep; it happens whether we're watching or not. But if we're awake, a sunrise can be a window to something larger.

A few evenings after this moment in the mountains, a group of longtime friends got together at our house. The topic of religion and children came up.

One friend said he has rediscovered the peace of church and hoped that he could communicate this to his children. He recalled his own childhood experiences at church as less than fulfilling; and the gap between what the adults said on Sunday mornings and what they did during the rest of the week did not escape him. Yet, he added, without his childhood exposure to church, he would not now find so much comfort in the rituals of liturgy and song.

Another friend hesitantly admitted that, because she has not introduced her children to organized religion, she feels guilty. She does not believe in religion herself, so she feels that taking her children to church would only teach them that parents are hypocritical.

And yet, this friend, who described herself as an atheist (she seems more of an agnostic), also remembers intensely spiritual moments as a child, moments when she believed she was speaking directly to a personal God. As an adult, she continues to experience what she calls peak experiences, when life becomes blindingly vivid.

As she described these moments, her face opened, her voice flowered. Our goal in life, she said, should be to recognize these moments, immerse ourselves in them, honor them, have more of them. I thought of my sons and the sunrise on the mountain. Such moments are the polar opposite of most of our days, when life seems robotic, when we stumble from deadline to deadline, pay the bills, grind through seemingly prerecorded conversations with our bosses and workmates and even our friends, when we fear that we will be detected for who we are, merely human. Whether or not we take our children to church, part of our role as parents is to guide them to recognize and appreciate these transcendent moments, these sudden connections with something bigger than worries or the world.

A few years ago, when a group of local religious leaders met in my living room, Rabbi Martin Levin, of Congregation Beth-El, said that to be spiritual is to be constantly amazed. "To quote the words of Professor Abraham Joshua Heschel, a great teacher of our age," he said, "our goal should be to live life in radical amazement. Heschel would encourage his students to get up in the morning and look at the world in a way that takes nothing for granted. Everything is phenomenal; everything is incredible; never treat life casually. To be spiritual is to be amazed."

For many people, organized religion offers the necessary structure, a weekly reminder that there is more to life and afterlife than budgeting and blackness. I have listened to the awesome silence of a church, and felt the meaning in the shadows. But since I was a boy, fishing has been my special window to the spirit. It is not the only window, but it is a good one.

On our recent fishing trip, I waded into the calm water, lifting the rod and letting loose of the line. I watched my boys along the shore. The younger one, who had given up on fishing, joyfully hauled his catch of the day, an old bucket, across the mud flats. The older boy had taken his rod into a thicket where there was a secluded pool. Perhaps, in that place, he was immersed in that quietest, strongest of voices.

Sometimes the rhythm of the rod is not unlike a chant or the swinging of incense. And sometimes you can feel the water, almost know beforehand that it will bulge beneath a fly. Mine did that now, and a big trout lifted from the surface, caught the sunset on its orange flank, and above the water stopped in time, as did my children and the world.

And then life went on. In a few hours, the boys and I would begin to miss their mother, and we would head home more amazed by the sunrise and sunset, by light and dark, by small muddy shoes on the stairs or the sound of my wife's hairbrush, by the smallest of moments.

Acknowledgments

I AM DEEPLY GRATEFUL TO MANY PEOPLE WHO, over the past decade, helped create the spirit of this book. For such a long stretch of time, there is no way to acknowledge all those who contributed. But among them were my family, Kathy and my two boys, Jason and Matthew. *The San Diego Union-Tribune*, its publisher Helen Copley, and its editors, present and past, Karin Winner and Gerald Warren, have provided me a homeplace from which to write. Most of the contents of this book are drawn directly from my column for that newspaper. Many hands-on editors nurtured this writing over the years, especially Peter Kaye, Jane Clifford, and Bill Osborne. Others of my fellow journalists, including Bill Stothers, Jon Funabiki, Matt Miller, David Mollering, Ellen Duris, Leigh Fenly, Randy Wright, John Muncie, Susan White, and others have given more time than friendship required. David Boe, my good friend, has listened to nearly all of these stories, and has donated his wisdom. Editor-in-chief Ann Pleshette Murphy, Bill McCoy, and my other editors at *Parents* magazine have given some of these thoughts a wider audience. I wish to thank Wayne Hilbig for his urgings, and Jackie Green for continued support. I am grateful to Anchor Books, Houghton Mifflin and Pocket Books, publishers of *Childhood's Future*, and *FatherLove*, from which a few selections were adapted. My assistant Shanna Dougherty was invaluable, as was Marie Anderson before her. My agent, James A. Levine, has provided moral and professional nourishment to this book, and even more to it's author. And I am grateful to Conari Press, a publishing house with the kind of values that sustain writers. Will Glennon, Emily Miles, and especially my editor, Mary Jane Ryan, helped stitch this work into a whole.

An Invitation from the author

Each of us is a weaver. Please share the ways that you find and give support—how you create a sense of connection among family, friends, community, nature, time and spirit. Send your thoughts and stories to:

Richard Louv
c/o Conari Press
2550 Ninth Street, Suite 101
Berkeley, CA 94710

or: rlouv@cts.com

About the Author

Award-winning journalist and author Richard Louv is a columnist for *The San Diego Union-Tribune* and a contributing editor to *Parents Magazine*. His ground-breaking books include *Childhood's Future*, which was excerpted as a cover story in The *New York Times Magazine* and the subject of a highly-acclaimed Bill Moyers PBS special, *Fatherlove*, *101 Things You Can Do For Your Children's Future*, and *America II*.

With appearances on *Good Morning America*, *The Today Show*, *Donahue*, NPR and numerous other TV and radio programs, Louv, who is a senior associate of The National Civic League, is a highly sought-after interviewee. He was a key participant in conferences on family issues moderated by Vice President Al Gore, and was asked by the White House to address the Domestic Policy Council at the first cabinet-level meeting on the issue of fatherhood. In 1994, he wrote *Reinventing Fatherhood*, a publication distributed by the United Nations to policy makers worldwide as part of the United Nations International Year of the Family. Also in 1994, he was asked by People to People to join a delegation to Russia to participate in the building of a new civil society in countries of the former Soviet Union.

In his columns, Louv writes about family issues, the environment, technology, cities, immigration, personal and public ethics, grass-roots politics, and renewal in American life. In addition to the *Union-Tribune*, his columns have appeared in *The Chicago Tribune*, *Christian Science Monitor*, *Cleveland Plain Dealer*, *Philadelphia Inquirer*, *San Francisco Chronicle*, *Charlotte Observer*, *Baltimore Sun*, *Detroit News* and many more newspapers.